The Hopeless Romantic

In Poetic Voice

with Guru Jah

A Word of Thanks

There are two individuals whom have been instrumental in what you are about to read.

The first of mention is Demi Stevens, founder of "Year of the Book," under whose inspiration I took up the challenge to honor my truth and create this book. Simply being around Demi insights an internal "I can do it" attitude for which she is known and brings to vast numbers of people.

Thank You Demi

The next of mention is Salvatore Marici. As he opened up with me, and began sharing his poetry, my vision of poetry changed. Therein I found great freedom of expression in the written word.

Thank you Sal

... Table of Contents ...

Introduction

Blessings there …

Thank you for your interest in exploring my visions and experiences; they are those of a "Hopeless Romantic." Put most simply, it is an outlook on life, an outlook on love.

I am amused in so many ways when I think of myself writing these works. As a young man, I had written a romantic poem that I chose to share with my father. He read it, and then turned to me saying, "That's great if your name is Francis Bacon, but it isn't". For decades then, my inclinations to write such works as these lie upon a very distant back burner; that is until the late nineties.

It was at that time I began writing again in earnest. Four poems included herein were from my first released work, "Awakening: Perceptions of Empowerment". In fact, the very first poem, "The Hopeless Romantic Me", was the inspiration for the entire last chapter of the book; I named that chapter accordingly.

They were all cut though since hopes of finding an agent were riddled with "no poetry" as though it's something vile. Once the book was completed, those four poems no longer seemed to have a place in that writing so they are contained here.

Though my writing continued, poetry lay dormant as a tool of self-expression; that is, until 2012; love enraptured

me on a whole new scale. It was the year of meeting
Lisa, a long overdue past-life reunion that ultimately led
to recovering a missing piece of my soul. That meeting
rekindled The Hopeless Romantic.

Poetry seems to have changed a lot through time;
at least from my exposure to it. As a kid in school, it was
always about rhymes; sometimes that seemed to outweigh
the message. Some of the works included in this book
utilize rhyme and some follow a rhyming meter. But some
do not; they are actually written in prose but clearly with
a poetic voice. Others yet, are far more freeform as
influenced by Sal.

I have always had a different view of love than
the collective conscious of mankind; these works, share
that view. Some may serve to validate what you already
experience and know in your heart; others may challenge
you at your deepest levels. I trust they shall lead you to
new horizons of looking at your own ideals about love.

Guru Jah here ...

One final Note

Poetry is to be read aloud.

Then again, my particular speech patterns may frustrate you on your first round of reading these works. Although I myself trip-up on occasion, the writings are in language I am personally comfortable speaking. I trust you will find my personal idioms not too disconcerting.

We typically will get the greatest understanding from a poem on our third or fourth reading; thus I invite multiple readings.

again, *Guru Jah here* ...

Let my voice be heard …

1

One whom did love me, albeit she confessed
only friendship, spent a day with me conveying her fears.
Fears, those doubts of mind created by others; but
sometimes the worst is doubting oneself.

I would dare to suggest that all our fears,
of others and self, are truly a lack of trust, self-trust.
Thus I wrote to her:

The Hopeless Romantic Me

Seldom in life have I known such treasures,
You touched my soul in greatest of measures.

A gift of love and the right to feel,
For once in my life, my soul feels real.

All that rejection, for to which I have cried,
The depths of that hell are pushed aside.

No fear, no hate, I'm accepted, I'm real,
From the depth of my soul, now I can feel.

A gift so pure makes the immortal man cry,
You lit upon me, as though a butterfly.

So innocent in spirit, so pure in heart,
The gift of your soul you do impart.

2

No greater wonder why so rare,
A world so blind; they do not care.

A spirit alive, changing flight with a start,
But that touch to my soul will never depart.

And what pray tell dare I ask of thee,
Only that you, shall always be free.

To clench my fist, afraid of the loss,
To crush your wings, such bastard thoughts.

Don't get me wrong, I would there be more,
In depth of my being, your truth I adore.

I thank the stars our paths did cross,
Having loved you is not a loss.

Your life's interactions, with souls in despair,
Love them all, yet on guard, that your wings do not tear.

Go in peace what directions you choose,
To pull at your spirit is only abuse.

You give so freely to all whom would care,
Despite *their* cries, there's no sin in self-repair.

Always a many will feel they did lose,
Seeing your gift, once past their blues.

Be yourself, see yourself, know who you are,
Trusting yourself will carry you far.

Thank you my friend
Guru Jah here ...

Finis

4

As I look about me in the world of man, at times I see how people feel trapped. I see their spirit and soul as lost and dead. It's a great part of why people seek to be entertained as such; it is their separation from life as an active participant. I began to wonder why; I began to look at what was different within me; and thus I write:

Passion

Passions rise and passions wane
To hold them close seems in vain

Some call it a cycle; some call it a tide
Yet we as adults do not abide

Muddled hopes and muddled dreams
Passions aplenty as broken schemes

But a child is free, they live not in fear
Embracing their passion, they know as dear

They believe in themselves, they follow their dreams
They fill their lives with *all* their schemes

But we come along and say it is wrong
We pick up the pieces and teach them *our* song

Yet we are blind to our own truth
We forgot what we knew in our youth

That driving force, no limits to bar
Passion's sweep carries us far

Conquering all we never fail
Now the mundane to feel pale

For just that moment, we know the glory
Our hopes and dreams true our story

Then of love, that's passion too
Our very lives it does undo

Rational sense we blow away
Trusting passion to make the day

All this I know, downfalls and all
Despite its truth, I follow the call

To live without passion I refuse to know
In balance with it, I do reap and sow

To find no passion in that which I do
Leaves me no reason and leaves me blue

It's a hellish trap borne day by day
To find new passion along the way

Just a spark, that wanting of flame
It sets us free, albeit insane

Liken new buds bursting in spring
Erupting ideals and love it brings

But then like the tide, that inseparable death
Like winters freeze, how it robs our breath

Disinterest sets in and pains our heart
We watch our passions soon depart

A hopeless romantic will be inclined
To live this cycle a million times

Without the force of passion I dear
I have no life; nothing comes near

It's not about superficial joy
It's not about a girl and boy

It's how we live life, and how we grow
Feeling our passion and letting it show

Naught is eternal in a static way
Everything changes day by day

Passion therein is the beauty
It's life itself, my call, my duty

Reckon away the ebb and flow
Our passion dies albeit slow

Cry as you will to limit the world
But not for I, for by life I'm hurled

A hopeless romantic you may say
But I live by change every day

Finis

We gather together in exploration of our connection with one another through ritual; we see the strands of our lives woven as one. Through this night is a bonfire with drummers and dancing; it is all in celebration of life.
It was of this night I write:

My Morning Star

Sitting atop the mound, beneath the web of unity, and watching, below me, my children danced. The celebration of life played out in intense rhythm to the beating drums. The fire they encircled reached high into the night as it released the living energy transformed; energy now embraced by those whom danced it. Each beat of the drum, each spark that flew, each step of their dance, they all became as one.

My children, they are the babes of the way. Many are as witches and lovers of life; most are just those of soul, wanting to grow. Far and between, one of the way may appear, but most are fouled in their own ego drawn near.

As a man seated there, it is lonely; as a warlock*, it is lonelier yet. By the powers within and about me, one such as I dare not proceed amongst only those of soul; those whom are not yet ready for the truth of my being. Whence the time is right, my soul, my flesh, joins my children as one.

10

Consciousness disappears into the abyss of time; ego amongst those of the way begins to diminish in presence of truth, in presence of power. Ever so slowly, the being of each is shown, their nakedness in body and soul.

Amidst this time of inner revelation before all to see, the most pure glow as bright as the fire's ember. Whence then again, did this one brilliant point of light come forth. As before, this one of pure essence stood apart from the mass.

As a pure manifestation of her goddess did this one shine. At times, she is encumbered by common leaches to her being; yet no utterance of belittlement, nor greater than thee did pass from her lips. She spoke only love, only caring, only acceptance; yet, she too, knew the lonely-ness; she too, as a woman, as a witch.

Though my holding of wisdom by way of the ancients is strong, the powers of this goddess witch were far more pure. She bore innocence with love as one of the way.

For those of us on this plane of existence, our human being is weighted. Our powers and sight are beyond that of mortals; we are the least likely to embrace the richness of living as one with another human being. Each unto their own kind do the human animals come unto one another; but for us, much as the stars of the heavens, no two shall be as one.

This night from the knoll as my spirit watched, the essence of her being yet again struck forth. Of all that danced, she alone held the magick in each movement of her body. She alone had climbed beyond this earth into the Oneness. Thus, as any man must give praise, so did I. Honor of more than human, honor before a witch, a true and pure witch.

With humility did my words bid praise due her. Then as required before a goddess, my presence did bow in departing. Thus alone was an honor to have had audience before her. Thus was the best of expectations for this time and place.

Through hours of dance and pulsations to the beating drums, I became entranced as one with the burning fire; the night wore on. Those in gathering, thinned in number. It came to pass that my body fatigued and fell to the cool grass for a moment of rest.

There upon the velvet skin of mother earth I lay; my eyes fixed into the heavens stars. Far from the earth was my soul in this moment of time. Thus, I noted not the approach of what was to be the most miraculous of encounters. The very one and same goddess did come forth to sit at my side.

Of whence conversation began, I cannot recall; it was more as speaking from the soul without words. Then for rhyme of reason unknown, my hand stretched forth to touch her face; it was more like unto an understanding than anything else; it bore nothing of earthly desire. To music unheard but felt by both, with each stroke of the palm and fingers about her head, our spirits danced.

Thus, it came that her burdened soul did seek rest and understanding. The burden of our kind, it is of isolation; it is of a difference from mankind despite our human form; we are human, yet not. Our kind, caring for those whom shall never reach our plane in their life cycle; we are born into mankind, yet never one with it. Then the pain, that of trying to be as one with mortals lives as an ever-turning cycle.

So then did her head and shoulder lie upon my chest. To be held, to be close, to be as one in full understanding. To be protected as it were from those who do not know, and never will. To be free of the loneliness; nothing is more painful than to lay with one and feel the loneliness; such was not the embrace of these moments.

About our unity formed a sphere of peace; much as though nothing else did exist for it did not. Eternity passed; yet in the blink of an eye came the intrusion of the golden threaded earthly being. He is one of soul, wanting to grow, so desperately, so inadequately; he had come with her; yet I noticed him not against her great essence.

Thus did the sphere burst, yet not the Oneness. She then turned to sit against my humanness; and this tender goddess allowed my enveloping presence. Now with her back to me, was I as one with her by my embrace. Arms wrapped around her torso, and legs straddling hers did we sit as one whilst the earthly being sat in awe.

13

Language now did become more prevalent, whence before it mattered not.

So very close we were, as no prior difference had ever been; no part of one was alien to the other; flesh upon flesh, spirit within spirit, being all as one. An hour or two had passed though unable to mark the time. It was ecstasy as one, with one of my own ... as one, with one of her own.

No words that I could scribe, could tell all of as it was. The warmth of her pure being, her pure soul, her purity as one with her goddess, did touch my every sense; breathing in her essence left her smell upon my taste. My body held her glow of warmth as from within myself; arms and legs were as though nonexistent.

Was it the cool of the morning air or the human distraction caused by the other? Never coming to know, we moved by the fire; somehow, in that move, the spell of Oneness was lost. As though the orbit of our predestined paths did call forth a separation; we parted. Time that once stood still began running rampant. The golden threaded one yanked his thread more like an umbilical cord yet uncut; humanness threw itself as a vast space of nothingness.

Amidst that break of dawn, she returned to her goddess being, a lonely witch; her dance began about the fire, she had returned unto herself. I found myself split between man and warlock. The human of me did cry for more; the warlock knew the magick he had held; so then did I turn and walk away.

14

These days past, my questioning has run deep. Was it then the man whom wanted more as led by phallic desire; or rather, the lonely existence of my being? Despite the query, the answer is known. My soul, my very essence shall always be in need to be as one with another of my kind.

To melt into her more fully; to dance the heavens as one would then have seemed to fulfill my quest. Yet, no matter how truly magickal the moment could have been, such would have come to its end. So then shall it be, what magick was held was all it could be.

The memory of that time; a blink of the eye in my eternity, shall remain so very precious. When asked, "How shall I know thee?" … Her answer, "I am Star, how many stars are there?" Truly then she is. As the morning dew glistened by the light, my morning star was gone from sight.

My eyes shall look for you in the heavens my little star. By chance of the ever-turning wheel, might my soul be blessed again by your presence I shall know bliss; and yet the blessing already given shall always remain. The pain held, day to day, softens in my memory of you, the part of you that penetrated me. Thank you little one, my morning star, blessed be.

*(The term "Warlock" as used here is with reference to a male witch, sometimes thought of more as a magician. Its usage is from the nineteen-fifties and early sixties;

current trends are to consider this term undesirably
meaning an oath breaker. Such is not the use herein.)

Finis

There are great truths of our being that I honor.
Among them is that we are what we think we are; it's often
a battle between our own truth and what others call reality.

If we think we are sickly, we are; if we think we are
healthy, we are. If we think we are unworthy, we are; and
if we think we are worthy, we are. Then it struck me, a
hopeless romantic … and thus I write:

Thoughts to Think

Surely it seems our thoughts are we
So then I question my thoughts of me
My truth seems simple and plain to see
But then to share love, how can it be

To ideals attached I've few at best
My held expectations are even less
So what guides my life so empty a quest
Naught to share love like all the rest

Do I think too much in my mind alone
Do I simply see love as some gilded throne
I've stumbled a lot, that's how I've grown
Yet the taste of love, *yes,* that I've known

I live of my truth and my ideals
It keeps me true, it makes me real
I walk as a human, I can even feel
But what does it take to make love real

If my thoughts of sharing are too abstract
Is it that alone that negates living fact
To share with another is a glorious act
Surely that truth a wight would attract

But then of others, how it makes them feel
They say they like it, that it holds appeal
They come around and share the ideal
But they never stay long to make it real

Shall I surrender what I know is true
A lie just to make we, a me and you
As I live my life that will never do
To greater truth I must be true

To live as mundane a separate being
Keeps us apart, truth never seeing
It locks us in fear, our heart ever fleeing
The way of the world, *their* way of being

So then of hopeless, a thought or a fact
Is my mind creating a one way track
My truth for me is my personal pact
In Oneness I live, in Oneness I act

I laugh at myself, it's all just a label
Hopeless, a word, denying I'm able
We preach that thought, a long lived fable
Myself I would share, my heart on the table

People may taste and then run away
For them it's a game, it's all a play
I'll live by *my* truth, with that I will stay
To be hopeless no more? Well, maybe someday.

Finis

During a period of my life, I had no romantic involvements in any manner. Seeking one had proven a farce; thus, it was a time to look within and feel sure what I might afford to such a being. What does it mean for me to love and what is it that I really want?

In Appreciation

That you might come forth and share a bit of life with me, it is good. Should you come forth, there is no obligation to share more than that which you desire it to be.

That you might reach forth and physically touch my being, it is good. By thy living essence shall I pleasure. But, there is no obligation to accept me beyond that which you give.

Should you accept my physical touch, it is good. By thy acceptance in which my being is free to be true, shall I pleasure. But, you are not obliged to hold me.

Should you hold me, it is good. By thy embrace shall I pleasure. But, you are not obliged to lie beside me.

Should you lie beside me in peace or play, it is good. By your simple presence shall I pleasure. But, you are not obliged to sleep with me.

Should you sleep with me as I rest, it is good. By thy trust shall I pleasure. But, you are not obliged to lie there as One with me.

Should you decide to lie as One with me for this time and place, it is good. By our union shall I pleasure. But, you are not obliged to remain. You are free.

And should you decide to remain, it is good. But, you are not obliged to stay forever. Such is not of truth. Remain as it is good for you, you are not obliged for more to be.

Then should you decide to part from me, it is good. For I rest assured that in parting, it is good for you. I would there not be else for you. Anything less, is not good for me.

Stay if you will, go if you must. I stand honored, for all that you did share. Me here … just me.

Finis

Hopeless? Well, maybe. It is in the stillness that we see ourselves most clearly. Thus I write:

Fog

I watch people gather saying they're friends
I watch people caring and see how it ends
I see people sharing coupled as two
But why is it never, a me and you

I watch people, most all are alone
Dank and dreary, chilled to the bone
They may be sharing with someone else
Yet loneliness screams within themself

Then I see others, they are filled with life
Yet they too walk alone though blessed in rife
So I'm not but one in this lonely plight
It seems we wander an endless night

I feel like a ship adrift on the sea
Though humans do couple there is no we
Lost and alone in vastness of space
I wander forlorn by the human race

We've crowded this planet packed like rats
Living in tension as though chased by cats
We packed us so tight there's no room to breathe
Yet to share with another, how can I believe

Then comes a light that I do see
Could it be someone is seeing me
They blink their light into the night
I'm sighted, I'm seen, I know I'm right

We blink back and forth, a blink in the now
I dream we may dock or at least cross bow
The currents of the sea are cruel it seems
All my desires midway end like dreams

They are the same, they're just like me
Trapped and alone, cursed reality
Most will never say it, it's just the life we live
Adrift on the sea, with no one whom to give

So shall I be bitter and curse my life
Shall I play the game of drama and strife
If I cannot be me then what's the point
For as I am, the gods do anoint

The break of day does leave me blind
The brilliance of Ra, it fills my mind
I see a world that I am not of
Wantonly humans pretending to love

And so I'll wander this hopeless way
Trusting to share in my heart to play
There are others like me, there is no doubt
And perhaps yet someday I'll figure it out

Finis

The Universe led me to reunite with a love from a previous life; we met again at a gathering of like-minded people. It changed my life, and thus to her, I did write:

Are You Real?

All that wonder I did feel,
It makes me ask, are you real?
Of all I dreamt that could not be,
You blew my view of reality.

Are you real?

Now worse yet, how real am I?
Then I wonder, did I die?
Where am I? And then why?
This can't be me, it's a lie.

A corporeal being of flesh and bone,
Aches and pains now well known.
Blacken eyes from sleepless nights,
Rampant desire in endless fights.

The shell of a face, furrowed deep,
Lost and alone, the mirror did speak.
A touch to my cheek by my own hand
Broke me to tears, this cloak of a man.

Are you real?

Hugging past the pendant of glass,
It was there I lost my mass.
Of all I held I could no more,
I let things drop to the floor.

To kiss your feet standing there
With lookers on, I did not care.
To honor you, that you are,
It mattered most, all by far.

Into my being you did fall,
We as One despite it all.
Finding me on the other side,
Two beings open, open wide.

A yellow flower you brought to me,
And laid in my hand, your purity.
If ended there I'd be alright,
I could have slipped into the night.

Are you real?

Then the class that we would share,
I found expression that laid me bare.
In simple touch and movement there,
We opened wide and both aware.

We touched we swayed, we moved as One,
Our sacred journey had begun.
Nothing barred and nothing held,
Into each other, we did meld.

In perfect union our breath did flow,
It filled our space, made it glow.
We breathed each other, our breath as One,
Our blessed union had begun.

Far above that space we flew,
In simple joy we both knew.
In space I've dreamt but yet to see,
There was no me, it was we.

Existence made real
As though meant to feel.
How dare I ask,
Are you real?

Then the day the sun did set,
I felt the squirm, **No! Not yet!**
To reach for you I did not dare,
Lest my heart begin to tear.

Peace I found in pure delight,
Would only last through one night.
You reached to me most humanly,
Bearing truth, the rite of we.

My own constraints I could not bear,
Beyond the veil, I found you there.
The gods did honor that we are,
Within their realm, we are par.

Conjured as real, my hearts appeal,
You did appear, are you real?
We danced, we loved like none before,
Desire runs rampant. I want more.

Into hell I then did fall,
My screaming heart the only call.
To walk alone is now not right,
Yet I must, every night.

I see a world but I'm not there,
I can't find me anywhere.
Scattered and shattered by my own hand,
I stand alone upon this land.

Swirling up to out of sight,
Are colored wings of pure delight.
En massed as One before my eyes
They hear not my mortal cries.

For just a moment I'd been there,
Touched in love that we did share.
Beyond all known, but all I knew,
A flight as One, in me and you.

Are you real?

A pendular swing to the far extreme,
But now I ask, what can it mean?
The fall back down is force unreal,
Slapped on earth, is this real?

Once in balance I'm now undone,
Simply since we danced as One.
You've raised the bar of my ideal,
You changed it all, you made it real.

Or did I dream it,
Are you real?

I've shared before as best they could
Limits on love as though they should.
Left in the dust, what once was good,
I've marched alone for all that I would.

I've danced with gods in space divine,
They've blessed me well, this heart of mine.
I've danced as One within their space,
But never once in the human race.

Did you descend to make it real?
Are you here? Are you real?
I've been so close yet not in full,
You broke all that, you gave no bull.

Are you real?

I'm shattered and broken in a world so hard,
I piece me together, a bundle of shard.
A fall from grace to this damnable place,
Now I walk with the human race.

I know I'll correct, it is my way,
But it feels not real, not this day.
I shake my head and query why.
Am I mortal? Shall I die?

Are you real?

Then full circle, it's a lie,
That within me cannot die.
I've danced, I've breathed, I've shared as One;
All we are is not undone.

Self-doubt, self- torture, I'll endure it all,
I'll even survive that hellacious fall.
From where I am, it seems unreal,
It's hard to dream, it's hard to feel.

A distant light I cannot see,
Could it be a part of me?
Is it me or is it we?
At least I know what *can* be.

Are you real, how dare I ask?
Are you real, you wear no mask?

Alone as man, it is my plight,
Yet I know what is right.
Your life entwined, I have no place,
I walk alone this human race.

And then of those yet to come,
They will know they're not the one.
I'll not surrender what is true,
I'd need to find another you.

Bits and pieces come my way,
Treasures all, but none will stay.
How dare I cling to you, how dare I not?
Of all I want, we're all I've got.

Me shunting me, that you be free,
It's my twisted cope of reality.
I have a heart. I want to share.
But in my mirror, it's just me there.

Are you real?

I've suffered times like these before,
To that extent, it's just one more.
To love detached I've learned so well,
Yet unlike before, this greater hell.

In times before I lived a dream,
But now there's proof of that unseen.
I know it's real, I know it's true,
I know it all, because of you.

31

Knowing well my price to pay,
I'll pray again for another day.
That we may share I know not where;
It would not hurt if I did not care.

So then I guess I have to know,
You are real, you let it show.
I'll walk alone and hug a tree,
Perhaps I'll find a bit of me.

Thank you for being real.
The nameless me …

Finis

Sometimes in life, we spin in a whirlwind from our presence in the now to thoughts of our past. Most people live in the past but such thoughts seem alien to me. Thus as they came to my attention, I could not help but write:

To Those Who've Touched Me Deeply

Kristy Johnston, you sat upon my lap in pure innocence that only a six year old could. We had sunny days at recess on the schoolyard wall by the playground; that was our sacred space. Your little sister came by just to be there, just to drink in the joy we shared. You eventually even took me home to meet your parents; we were getting quite serious you know. I remember those days with smiles upon my face and joy in my heart.

I remember sitting on the floor in my bedroom, making you that necklace of candy beads as a gift. I remember you happily wearing it. But then came the loss of our innocence, the loss of love shared. That older fat girl, I remember her too; the one that ripped that necklace from your neck. Her words so long ago escape me now, but that's just as well. Though I scrambled to collect all those scattered beads, they could never be the same.

It was her anger in jealousy that changed my world; I saw then the human horror. Somewhere after that day, I lost you Kristy; I lost innocence, I lost the experience of love. Had the fat girl never come by, I can only wonder

33

what further impact you might have had on my life. But now, these many decades later, I can at least say thank you Kristy, your innocent love was a joy in that time and space; you touched me deeply.

Joan Prepstol, you caught my interest in the youth group at church, but it wasn't there that we found room to feel inspired by one another. It was the afternoon parties at your house on summer days that stick in my mind. We danced, we felt free and alive; and eventually, you let me catch you in a chase to give you a kiss. What a shock to my being; I could not do it; I froze like ice on a winters day.

It had nothing to do with you, you were perfect, my very ideal. In those days, I had yet to overcome my devastated self-worth, all so damaged by the world around me. What a loss; a chance to share love as best we knew how, blown by the wrath of other people. Yet I remember the inspiration through you to be alive, your joyfulness and laughter, your smile, the dance of light in your eyes. I even remember those lips I felt unworthy to kiss; they bore a slight scar, but they and you were perfect. Thank you Joan; for a short time until I froze and lost you, I knew joy; you touched me deeply.

To the girl in senior art class, long blond hair below your waist, I feel silly; I cannot remember your name. You were the first to touch my soul as though I knew you from time before; your presence stopped me in my tracks. You captivated me like no one else; we could talk, but not much else. You let me walk you home one day and carry your books; well, sort of to your home.

You bid me that I part at the railroad tracks lest your parents would see and object; they lay heavy upon you. I always knew that life had not been kind to you; but we could never seem to cross that barrier; I lost you at that railroad crossing. You came too close for your own comfort. But I thank you for coming as close as you did; for that little bit, I felt really connected; you touched me deeply.

Kathy Uhler, oh my dear Kathy, what a mistake I made. Every time I would be in your presence, it was a joy. And the best part, I'd dare to say you found me desirable to some extent; possibly for even more than what little we did share. I still smile with memory of playfully trapping you against the wall in the school hallway. You told me you'd scream rape, but you bit your tongue by my reply. "Go ahead, but if you do, I may as well do it because I'll get in trouble for it whether I did it or not."

But oh my error; often I muse what direction life may have taken. I walked to the cafeteria table with intent of asking my girlfriend-of-sorts to the senior prom. Thinking she would be the one to respond, I announced, "I'm going to the senior prom, would anyone like to come with me?" It floored me that four others there raised their hand; but the one that shocked me most was you. I'd dare to say your hand flew up the fastest. That girlfriend-of-sorts, she never did raise her hand; I almost had to twist her arm.

During it all, I kept looking back at you, churning inside with delight that you would go with me. I still can see your excitement, and your disappointment. But after all, I came to ask someone I'd been seeing for some time now, how dare I? So I blew it Kathy, I really should have grabbed that opportunity. Instead, I took a young lady that I eventually married; but now that's old history of shattered dreams. But in my memory, there are smiles and a game of "what if;" what if I had dared to take the girl that left me feeling like a million bucks. I assure you Kathy, doing it over, you would be my pick; even if that prom were the last of it. Thanks for that game worthy memory; it delights me; you touched me deeply.

Anne Laure, when I come to name you amongst these who touched me most, I'm almost at a loss for words; your touch went beyond that. It was you that brought me back to the truth of love. It was you that penetrated my very soul. It was you that reminded me what joy could be. It was you that led me back to looking at life with the innocence of a child.

You showed me your joys, your sorrows, your truth. I got to experience love as a joy, far more than just a comfortable relationship. I always felt like we were sharing something; we were sharing each other; even though you insisted, "we were friends". It was never a matter of pre-tense; it was always being real as who we were to each other and ourselves. Your smile, your hugs, your laughter, and even your times of turmoil, I remember them with delight.

Had the time in your life been right, I muse that we might have shared so much more. And, I seem to know there was more; we just never got there. You were always fearful of yourself and your love for me. As friends? Well, maybe. Amidst your failing marriage and forbidden love of yet another, it was a blessing you loved me at all. Yet to share, and to love, it is in your nature. You afforded me a human aspect of love that was real; and for that, I thank you endlessly. But then again, sending you a long list of thank yous ended our sharing, dare I say it was timing?

It was then that I lost you; you went away. I know you had to; life was beating upon you without mercy. I tried to look you up a year or two ago; I had no idea Anne Laure was such a common name. But the faces didn't look right. Maybe you have changed that much; I guess I have in all these years. What was missing though in those photos was the dancing light of your eyes; none of them had it; they could not be you. Or, has the world beaten you up that much? I trust not. Maybe that dancing light of your eyes was something most never got to experience; but I did; it brought me joy. Thank you for touching me so deeply.

Jessica, we approached one another so slowly at first. But, once past the initial hesitation, our union descended to dance as One on this plane. Just standing there you kissed my feet in a way only the divine know; you blessed me. To speak the language of the ancients with you felt so right. We shared a spiritual connection, far beyond just human.

I remember you as a dynamic force playing out your role here in full truth of your being. I remember you coming over to ask if I were smoking, altogether thankful you could no longer smell it every time I lit one up; smelled no matter how far away. To this day, I am honored to have embraced such Oneness with you.

At our second uniting, time shared I'd thought an hour, proved out to be four; in space with you, time held no relevance. Though I'll probably never see you again lest I travel to England, I can always feel that space with you. By that memory, you have blessed me well; you brought me joy, and I thank you. You touched me deeply.

Lisa Tice, you too are hard to write of. You risked it all and rode off with me to the unknown; that was brave. The Universe threw us together almost as if without option; lucky for me, you embraced it. You brought to me something unique; it was the capacity for love, a capacity on all levels. To embrace you was to embrace the innocence, the humanness, the spiritual essence, all at once. You changed my life for this is love as I remember it. Knowing this capacity for love is no longer an obscure memory.

You and I are no strangers to this; we have shared in this capacity before, centuries ago. Perhaps hence the reason we were directed with such force. I remember you commenting on the empty centuries past; but at that point, I had not grasped the full magnitude of its meaning. Lifetimes, including this one, of never feeling fully loved have plagued me hard. You broke all that.

Now I remember what it feels like to be touched. Not just in joyful innocence, in warm humanness, or in spiritual uniting, but all, all at once. You gave that touch with physical presence, but there was more; it was energetic too. I remember watching you sharing your love in full trust of yourself; sometimes it was with others to a point, but especially with animals, you shared yourself to a far greater level. You trusted yourself to that greater level with me too, at least a couple of times. It was not simply your loving heart, but your loving essence; it is far more magnificent than just your heart. In that space, your heart and your essence unite. For that, I thank you.

You brought me joy; and yet, oh my, you brought me internal conflict in so many ways. Our time together beset by your need for space left me constrained; but it was good, for I watched you become more whole unto yourself. It amazed me how hard it was to walk away from you when our time was done; but it was. At least our parting led me to the trail of resolving that centuries old curse I had placed upon myself. Reclaiming that missing piece of my soul was important to me; so was the repair of my heart. I am finally free to embrace love wholly; in that, you have blessed me beyond compare and I thank you. Had you not reached out, had I not heard the voices of the Universe and followed, that time we shared would never have been. You touched me deeply.

As I scribe these words, it is a look back at times of love in many ways. Yet those times are all fleeting, never to last. In fact, those who touched me most deeply are those with whom I never embraced in life as a partner. Partners have come and gone, each bringing something in their time. I can suppose that was good, but only good. To be touched deeply holds far greater delight.

These that touched me, I lost as such. Of course, that is lost, only if one can presume that I had anything more than a simple passing of ships in the night. So then, is this the old saying, "It is better to have loved and lost than never to have loved at all"? Is it that the greatest of love is always transitory, always illusive? Or is this simply the reminiscing of an aging man? The voices though, they are speaking of something different.

I hear the call of desire, the desire to love in its need of self-expression. Surely, love unexpressed is useless, sometimes even painful in our erroneous attachment to it. Desire though is the polarity, the possibility, the potential; and when touched, it is alive and poised for passion. Passion drives the Universe. All creation is in the arc of polarity discharge; *that* is passion. *That* is its magic. Nothing in the Universe is stationary, unmoving; that is unless it is dead. Now the message becomes clear.

Memories of love lost, even when not fully expressed, are indeed the most precious and enlivening. They did not die; they simply ceased opportunity in the Now. When embracing love until its death, we lose passion, and we can even lose desire. Without desire, we ourselves have died. Those of supposed religious enlightenment denounce desire; they are silly. Desire is the polarity of the Universe. If desire dies, the Universe becomes un-manifest, and so do we.

What seed without desire will ever see the outside of its shell? What plant grows from a seed without passion? Thus, do I invite desire into my being, into my essence; for then I am alive and poised for passion. Desire, you have blessed me well and I thank you; you touched me most deeply.

Finis

Upon experiencing love to a degree I thought impossible on this earth, it came to pass that I looked in the mirror and saw a difference in me, a difference in my vision, a difference in how I saw life. Such love had only existed as "hopeless". Thus I write:

You Set Me Free

Oh so much do I thank thee
You have come and set me free
Free to love
Free to be

I have never feared death
It mattered not to me
In so many ways, so was life
I have walked in life simply accepting it

And it has been good in many ways
There have even been times of great joy
I had come to peace with life
Yet it was always born by indifference

But now, now there is a difference upon me
Now, I want to live, I want to experience it
Now I want to share in life and be
Thank you Love, you set me free

Finis

Sometimes as we embrace a loving relationship, our sharing can become stressed as we see the differences between each other. A young woman with whom I shared life became increasingly entangled in seeing those differences; they tugged at her mind and heart, bringing her displeasure. Thus to her I wrote:

Our Tapestry

The threads of our lives are entwined together liken the threads of a fine tapestry.

Individual yarns may vary in color, brightness, and visibility. Held one against another a clash of differences may seem to prevail, their essence irreconcilable.

Yet, by virtue of life as these strands weave their way through the daily ups and downs, ins and outs, the discernible pattern that is woven is a masterpiece of creation.

No single element of our existence together may display the whole of our being. We are made as us by the inter-locking of each and every part of our varied fibers.

Let us not dwell upon the contrasts of any given thread as though its presence is more unwanted than that of a weaver's knot. Individually our strands are weak and would bear little stress. Interwoven unity bestows longevity.

Having not the knowledge of our creations intent, our variegated threads may seem as though out of our control; it's a universal fear. Strands of such diverse colors make up our individual existence.

Our real control lies in our desire to share and our willingness to surrender any perception of the pattern by the hands of the weaver.

Our tapestry is one of a kind, the very element that is consistent with value and ultimate desirability. Our pledge to one another can be nothing more, and nothing less, than to share and to surrender.

Such a vow is not to subjugate our individual threads, but rather to glory in their union and entwinement. We need fear not as to change our colors nor hide them beneath the multiple layers of yarn.

We are that we are, and great in that. But the union of us, is the greatest of all.

Finis

So often in spending time with women of romantic interest to me, it ends up that I'm simply listening; listening to all their stories. I suppose that many men are the same in telling their tales; I don't really know.

What strikes me is that they are only sharing their cookie crumbs left along their path; seldom where they are in the Now and where they are going. Be those crumbs sweet or sour, take them away, and people are lost; they lose themselves in the past. Thus I write:

Now

Live in the past and not the Now
Desiring to share, I ask you how

Sharing only where you have been
In being with me is very thin

As you speak and share your thoughts
Be you with me, or past begots

If you are your past for nothing new
It makes me wonder how you grew

If you're not here and only there
It leaves me ponder for what you care

Are you with me or someone past
Is this your way of making *that* last

Must we unpack baggage of old
All kept live by stories you've told

Where are you amidst that tale
In finding you, I seem to fail

You tell me person, place and thing
But naught of feeling did it bring

Feelings of old are emotions now
Buried deep, no place for *wow*

Wow to me is what *we* might share
Feelings alive and laid to bare

Living the Now in its full glory
Gives little room for just old story

Your very presence, it is a gift
But without *you* present leaves a rift

The greatest gift that you might give
Is sharing Now that *we* might live

Finis

47

When two people come together and spark the magic of sharing, there is often a period of waiting. There are so few of us alive in the Now so fully that a spark can manifest as fire without smoldering first. Often it is simply cleaning up loose ends of life we once knew.

There came a time of waiting to share with one whom desired to share life with me. She had forewarned me she would bring her life in full, including her stuffed elephant; she would come forth as though never to go back. Yet, amidst it all, she was unsure she would embrace "our" time to share at all. We were relegated to only emails for months upon end. In sharing my truth, I then wrote to her:

Waiting to Share

okay, bull ... yeah, I'm screaming but laugh at
    my own insanity
I miss you
I want to share with you
I want
I want
I want

patience Jah, it shall come in its time
**I want to reach right through this damn screen
    and pull you through it**
patience Jah, it shall come in its time

elephant and all
patience, patience, patience, patience, patience …
I know if I write it enough, I might accept it, patience,
         patience, patience ...

let it go?
nope
desire run rampant
we
how beautiful
sharing
how beautiful
you
how beautiful
me too
how beautiful

patience?
it sucks
patience Jah
how can I be patient?
I am driven
I am consumed
I am insane
I am another as One

I know love
I can share love
I can feel love from another
I can experience love from another
I can experience love *with* another

49

patience?
patience or surrender?
to which?
to love shared?
or waiting?
I know waiting
I know it well

to love truly shared
that is new
that is powerful
that is a blessing beyond what I thought could ever be
patience?

no Jah
honor what *is*
honor what *may be*
even if it is not the I want
even if it is not what *we* want
even if it is what we *must(?)* accept

how can I love if I cannot accept?
I can't
therefore I must accept
patience Jah

patience
share what is real, that is love
it is love we share
so why shall I scream?

I scream because for once, just for once
    I really want to experience living
it is no longer borne with indifference
I could not slip into the night
into the darkness

there is light within me
and *we* share it
there is light within you
and *we* share it

and that is love
and that is bliss
and that is ecstasy
and that is joy
and I want
and you want
and there is *we*

patience, or honoring?
is there a difference?
yes, I honor
patient for the 99.99% that *we* may be
honor if the .01% doubt prevails

I honor you Love
no matter what
I honor you

Finis

Often as I lie to sleep, the Universe bestows me with visions, visions of a greater truth. As I watch these visions unfold it is important to let them run their course that I not adulterate the messages I'm given. Often then, I'm not sure what is unfolding before me until it's done; and sometimes not until the next day.

This vision was clear almost immediately. A past life scenario of love had entangled my life for many months, physically, emotionally, even spiritually. Healing work had been immense and a sense of completion had set in; this vision confirmed it. Only now am I able to write:

That Deadly Game

The yellow sphere before my eyes,
Confuses me; I wonder why?
Then it comes and now I see,
A burning fire inside of me.

Manipura in molten heat,
Destroying me, myself complete.
Arms outstretched and open wide,
Myself laid open, it's how I died.

From my smolder the bird arose,
Flying hard, his passion grows.
The flash of light exploding me,
Caught him too, left razed debris.

His tri ringed eyes and crown of plume,
Fell to ash as though be ruin.
Into an egg he did fall,
Formed about him, covered all.

Speckled spots of gray and blue,
Protecting he; but I bear the shrew.
Into the sea, an abyss deep,
He's cradled now as though asleep.

I drink the sea until it's dry,
I hold him close for he is I.
My soul surrendered escaped from me,
I take it back and make it we.

Separate chill be made warm,
This new life I thus form.
Hatch my soul and be free,
Welcome back to walk with me.

I played the fool in another's name,
I died for her, yet I'm to blame.
I loved me less, even truth,
I see me then, impetuous youth.

Centuries later and wiser now,
My soul returns, it fills my brow.
I stand for truth and stand for me,
I now stand whole for all to see.

Even her, she comes again,
Yet misplaced love, has met its end.
I love her still, but not the same,
I will not play that deadly game.

Finis

It's not uncommon for me to be excited in life; in ways it's even considered manic by those who need to classify such behavior. I awoke this morning in such a state, bouncy and excessively happy; somehow I could only see myself as an excited playful puppy. It was nearing a time when I'd be able to share with a dearest of love. Thus I shared my enthusiasm with her as I wrote:

Puppy Love

Are we here yet?
Huh
Huh
Are we here yet?
And when we get here
Do i have to behave?
Do i have to hold back?
Can i just be me?
Can i wiggle and waggle?
Can i be all excited?
Oh
Maybe not
Why?

Are we here yet?
Huh
Huh
Are we here yet?
Sure seems like we ought to be
This trip just can't last that long
And when we get here
Do i have to be on a leash?
That be-a-good-boy collar really chokes me
Can i just promise to be good?
Oh
Maybe not
Why not?
Huh
Huh

Why aren't we here yet?
I just want to jump up and let my paws land
           where they may
They're clean
Honest
They were just washed
In a mud puddle
It was clean
Sorta

I just want to run in circles around your feet chasing my tail
Oh
You might trip
Well
Suppose i run circles around just one foot?
Would that work?
I promise to not get so excited i pee on your feet
Well
Maybe

It's hard to promise what i'll do in excitement
It's been a long time since i've had any accidents
But it's been a long time away too
If i catch my tail and bite too hard i might pee
If i bite your fingers instead is that okay?
Oh
Maybe not

Do i really have to be good?
So when are we here anyway?
Huh
Huh
Huh
So when are we going to be here?
Oh drats

Do i have to stay locked up in this travel cage?
It's nice and all, but it's still a cage

When we get here, can i get out?
Oh, but then do i have to be good?
Is that why i'm in this cage?
If i pee in the cage, would you feel safe i'll not pee
        on your feet?

Are we here yet?
Huh
Huh
Did we miss the turn?
Are we lost?
So why aren't we here yet?
Huh
Huh
Huh

Oh
If i act too excited, i may have to wear that leash
That sucks
Big time
Then i might not be able to lick your face
i promise not to slobber
Well
Maybe i can promise
i could try to keep it to just one or two licks
i could try to keep them little licks
Well
Maybe

That might be hard to do
But if i do slobber
i can just lick that too
It'll all feel the same to you
Oh
Maybe not

i don't like the leash
That collar hurts
Who invented that anyway?
Are we here yet?
I know we're close
It's gotta be just around the next bend
i can feel the excitement building

Oh
Excitement
i may have to pee
If i don't drink any water i wouldn't pee on your feet
That may help the slobbering too
Then can i get out of the cage?

We must be here
Are we here yet?
Sure seems like we are
Well
No
I guess not
If we were
I might be chasing my tail
Barking happy yaps
Jumping all over
Making a mess
Oh
Hmm

Well if i just bark a little is that okay?
If i just bark i wouldn't make a mess
If i just bark i might not pee on your feet
And if i'm busy barking
i can't be licking your face
Would that be better?
Naw
It doesn't feel that way to me either
But do i have to be good?
Would yapping be better?
How about little yips instead of yaps?
Yips are good too
Then the neighbors might not mind

Are we here yet?
Huh
Huh
This sure is a long trip
We gotta be almost here
I like trips and all
Sorta
Kinda
Sometimes

Sticking my nose out the window is fun
It keeps my nose dry
So you see
When we're here
i might not slobber
Maybe
Well
Maybe a little
It's hard to tell
i might
Is that okay?
Oh

Are we here yet?
Huh
Soon i hear
Soon

The total irony of this piece, it turns out that the week before this writing, a new puppy had been brought into the house of that dearest love. This Saturday morning was a time of her extended playing with that puppy, all during   the same hours of my excited state.

Finis

So few understand Oneness, yet it's so simple.
In terms of human love, it's all I know as real; thus I write:

As One

I would that you lay beside me
I would that you lay inside me
And I would that I lay inside you

Me inside you, and you inside me
Then we are as One, it's easy to see
As our bodies exist, with it has little to do

Our dancing souls, it is how to be
United as One, in you and in me
Lay together separate, then *we* are through.

Finis

Sharing as One is perhaps the most beautiful experience I know of. Yet of late, I have seen it so misunderstood. Thus I write:

Joined

So often it comes that I see
People joined, they are *we*
In all they do and all they share
They are *we* beyond compare

To so many this life is bliss
Thinking all should be like this
His and hers matching sets
Even sharing little frets

Never separate in all they do
Their *we,* is all a me *and* you
No idea or feelings to own
For they are *we* to the bone

They've nothing to share that is not *we*
At least it keeps simplicity
Then I wonder if they share the John
Is it a two-seated toilet to sit thereon

They've lost themselves to the *we*
As though alone they could not be
No thought or care themselves to love
Ones divine essence they know not of

Joined at the hip may sound like fun
A three-legged life lived as one
The problem is there's no *you* to share
You can't be you, you'd never dare

Now when I say as One is right
In this sense my words are blight
To share as One means just that
It's sharing *ourselves* that melds in phat

Finis

65

My very nature is to walk in truth; it is by truth that trust is built. And of love, well, that too must be based upon truth; truth that begets trust. That is the foundation of love; it is the horse that pulls the cart; and so it must be. A dear woman came before me and the Universe showed me the way; thus I write:

A Matter of Trust

She comes to me in her need
Signs of trust are what I read
By all I see and infer
Her trust of me does much for her

By my desires and longing to share
I'd hop right in, but I do not dare
It must occur as though not I
Lest her trust she does deny

Like the leaves upon the trees
They must think they make the breeze
Her feeling empowered matters most
It must be I as though a ghost

That I never hold nor ever cling
My own demise that would bring
That I never impart desired intent
Lest her trust by that I spent

Cherish her essence, fill her void
Though my humanness be devoid
Such is this sharing as it must be
For how else can I, draw her, to me?

And who knows in time to come
She may loose her heart, be undone
And therein I might play
Ever thankful for that day

Finis

In my rounds of travels throughout the year, there are two gatherings in particular whose theme is sacred sexuality.

From my personal perspective, sacred sex is the uniting and expression of our spirit essence. The body and all the sexual expressions we experience only come along for the ride helping to expand that union.

By all means, not everyone attending those gatherings embraces such greater truth of sexual expression. But there are usually a few; they either embody the knowing, or at least are coming close. At a gathering past, a young woman came forth, and thus I write:

Why?

You hug me, and I hug you
You feel my essence through and through.
You know my being, and feel the "we"
It is I, inside you, and you, inside me.

There is no question of how or why,
Our sacred sex union does apply.
You speak it then later affirming it's true,
There was just we, no me, no you.

Sharing our spirit embracing as One,
Our sacred sex union had begun.
Beyond the ways of mortal man,
Our flesh and spirit both demand.

You yearned to hug for more than a year
To embrace that space you knew as dear.
But you held back, desire denied,
Expression in waste, your sacredness cried.

You speak there is no reason to not enjoin,
You hold no boundaries barring your groin.
Flesh to dissolve within our fire,
It is by this we could climb higher.

The spirit of desire then knows the way,
There is hope to share more this very day.
To enjoin the body along the way,
In sacred sex, we might play.

My door stands open that you might seek,
Yet through the night, you never peek.
Instead, you go to another tent,
And there your sex of flesh is spent.

Why?

I sense your fear of knowing more,
Afraid to share what you adore.
Embracing heights beyond the flesh
Brings mortal sex to its death.

Is your fear you cannot undo
The very sense of losing you?
For us to lay and be as One
Once engaged is not undone?

Laying alone it occurs to me
What it is then that you see.
Sex of flesh you can give away,
Sex of spirit you think must stay.

You fear attachment beyond desire,
Your freedom thrown to a funeral pyre.
For you to share the greatest of all
Leaves you destined for a heartfelt fall.

But for us to share then walk away
Gives room to share on another day.
Spirit essence does not attach
Thus human fears are no match.

Yet dwell as mortal if you must
Your fearful heart is what you trust.
I'll sleep alone and close the door
It's *sacred sex* that I adore.

Finis

Today, a question was asked of me; it horrified me.
And thus I write:

Do You Know I Love You?

When I come near, you talk all the time
Talking about you, it's all very fine

Shared words of me belittle and demean
Speaking your truth otherwise unseen
It's obvious to others you treat *me* mean

You question me, my being to defend
What, where and why to the bitter end
Once feelings of trust, now you do rend
Is this then the way, you treat a friend

Rebuking my acts shared from my heart
The gifts I then give become bitter-tart
My needs be unworthy, you verbally impart
I feel disrespected, right from the start
It leaves me thinking I'm not very smart

Amidst all this I do stand back and view
You think my stance taken is somehow new
You dare to suggest I find peace with you
Now you cry what we had leaves you blue
After all, our sharing has gone very askew
And now you ask, "Do you know I love you?"

No, I do not.

Finis

In a time enduring distance, hopes, and desire, the mind can run rampant, rampant to as insane, insane for love. Questions, even moments of fearful thoughts plague our being. I am no different. To one then who set before me such dilemmas, I wrote:

Unbridled Voice

Liiiiiiiiiiiiiiiiiiiiiiiiiiiiiisa
Liiiiiiiiiiiiiiiiiiiiiiiiiiiiiiiiiiiiiiiiiiiiiiiiiiiiiiisa
Do you hear me Love?
Do you hear my voice?
Do you hear my call?
Shall I whisper?
Lisa

We know you hear
I of the we, of the All
Are you resisting dear Love?
Is my voice driving you to madness?
Do you cover your ears
Trying to stay sane?
L_I_S_A_A_A_A_A_A_A

The other gods
They carry my voice
You cannot escape
Would you to escape?
Is it a trap?
Does my voice bind you?
Does the call of your name
Drive you insane?
Lisa

I am love
I am that you desire to know
I am that you desire to express
I am that you desire to share
You too, are love

You too, dwell the unmanifest
We both have
We walk time uncounted
Thus I whisper in your ear
Lisa, Lisa, Lisa

Shall I be reduced to will over will?
Must I command?
Must I demand?

Eternity is on my side
I am the void
I am the potential of will
That power is within me
Lisa
Must I
Must I really be reduced?
Must I release that will
Let it run rampant upon this earth
Must I destroy everything that restrains?
Everything that denounces sharing love
Lisa

Must I hold my tongue?
Must I speak not?
Lest in that I command
Must I hold my mind?
Lest my thoughts alone command

Must I abstain the very Truth?
Truth of the Universe
That it express itself
That it manifest
That it grow
I am the Universe
I am love
Lisa, Lisa, Lisa, Lisa

It *is* a trap
If I speak not
You may not hear
You shall hear only the echo of you own voice
That of you
Love that you would be
Love that you are
Truth of the Universe

The I of the All
We are patient Love
Time is only human
We only suffer it as human
Yet by you, I now would be human
By you, I now choose to express as human
Lisa
Yet I am that I am
You are that you are
Love
The expression of the Divine
The expression of the All
The All, expressing as One

Therein though, there in Truth
There is freedom
Truth is freedom
Thus from my will
Shall your name be moved
Thus from my mind
Shall your name be moved
Rather your name shall rest upon my heart
For my heart is open
It commands not
It demands not
It only invites
Lisa

Love
To share as One
That is love
It is we

To be in Truth
Is to be free

Therein too, is love
Accepting love is not to bind
Accepting love is to bliss
Expressing love is to bliss
Thus your name becomes bliss
I embrace bliss

It is love
It is Truth
It is we
Lisa, what a joyous sound
It dances upon my heart
Upon that plane
It dances to song
The song of your name
Hear not my voice
But hear the song
Lisa ♪♫♪

My heart invites you to hear
My heart invites you to share as One
My heart invites you to be you
Love that is you
It is Truth
It is free
It is open
Share the dance when you are ready
Soon Love
Soon

Soon by your own voice
In wanting to share
In wanting to love
Lisa, soon

Finis

I always look at my inner-self; it's part of knowing oneself. We can hardly accept and appreciate what we do not know. And then I laugh with what words I might use to convey my truth of essence to others. My question to me, what does it mean for me to be the "Hopeless Romantic"? Thus I write:

Alas

And so say I, I live my days in love,
Silly me, what does that consist of?
Romantic flings, a wild passion night,
A marriage of two, as though that's right?

Truth be known, it's all just me,
My twisted sense of reality.
To share with a human, desire I do,
Seeing as One, the me and you.

Then in that space I see it all,
A being of One into we'd fall.
But who am I fooling, who do I kid,
There's no one here, no you to bid.

My days in love, is it a joke,
Is it at me, this fun I poke?
Yet say I, I've loves aplenty,
Then I wonder, just how many?

I see them all, but they're not here,
So then I wonder, to whom is dear?
Each shares as One, to some degree,
To this do I cling, only fooling me?

My desire to share is always there,
Myself wide-open, my truth laid bare.
It shows in my eyes, it shows in my heart,
Open acceptance I give from the start.

Though I admit, I may *choose,* not to care,
Ill being energies, I'd rather *not* share.
But those who are true, and see as One,
That's when my heart, becomes all undone.

By chance as I find, those precious few
I would change my life, and start anew.
Over and over it happens to be,
They spark me to fire, igniting me.

Yet every time the fire burns out,
Despite it be real, beyond any doubt.
Reduced to embers in ashes of coal,
They lie in my heart, my very soul.

Then by chance as we meet once more,
Those embers burst, they stoke my core.
Once lying dormant, love expresses itself,
That unto which, I would share as though pelf.

But love unexpressed, what can it be worth,
A soul full of ember, love borne as dearth?
But I see love as much bigger than that,
A state of mind, it's a matter of fact.

Love is to *see* and know *all* is *One,*
Existing as many, *One's* never undone.
Embracing our essence is what makes life real,
Being and sharing as One, makes living ideal.

It's not to say there is no me;
It's not to say all must be we.
Though we exist in separate form,
That skin and bone is just adorn.

Be it rocks and trees, or the sky and breeze,
Or Mother Earth, they're as One, all of these.
Animals, spirits and fey, by all that exists,
We are all One, but with different twists.

Seeing this, feeling this and knowing this
Is the beauty of life, it is life's bliss.
As I then walk through life sharing all,
I can share love for there is no wall.

But then of humans, we separate so,
It all plays out in our mind and ego.
Control, expect, our feelings to hide,
Closing our hearts be narrow not wide.

Thus to find that beauty inside
Is a hellish task, it's an ugly ride.
All those by ego who choose to shield,
Their true essence comes never to yield.

But those that know their essence true,
Are open to share, in me and you.
My eyes all three are open wide,
To see what beauty *they* don't hide.

This earth then I walk, so humanly alone,
Yet despite all that, I will seldom bemoan.
For to come in truth, and be as we are,
Is the joy in sharing, greatest by far.

It is unto this, that I spend my days,
To experience love, in so many ways.
Those embers I honor, for each is alive,
They're part of my id, as my inner drive.

I trust that I'll find, so many more,
Those who live truth, those I adore.
It's not just a quest, as though I be whole,
It's more an expression, of my very soul.

By this then, with my eyes open wide,
Romantically I walk, warm and fuzzy inside.
After all, I might even find someone to share with.
It all may seem hopeless, that's okay, it's *my* myth.

Finis

One cannot experience the grandeur of love in the Now without sometimes catching ourselves in that our Now may be empty of human connection. To know the warmth of bliss, it serves us to know too, the chill. It all centers on that sense of connection and our desire to share, of which I write:

The Empty Night

It's late, almost midnight, yet I'm awake, awake and alone. Worse yet, I'm very awake, and the stillness is empty.

I'm free so they think, free to go anywhere, but this my home. Parked for the night in the midst of cement and closed stores.

People approach me during the day with wonder at my life. They speak of their traps, but somehow they never see mine.

From three hundred feet away one smiles as she approaches. She's not really attractive, but she's aware and alive.

She sees me and tells me of her, for she too loves the road. She speaks of seven years as a carnie with sparkle in her eyes.

She hugs me thrice and squeezes my hand in all her delight. Yet what she wants, "to be honest," is money to buy wine. 10am.

So my pocket is a little thinner, but it's okay, she seemed happy. But as the town closes down, all I can wonder is, am I, happy.

Was it worth the trade? Is it anything more than paying a whore? Even a whore goes away when she is done, everyone does.

And then, I'm alone. There aren't even bums to beg for money. And then of course, I can only wonder for what it is that I beg.

I turned away a beggar during this day in his cry of hunger. He wanted not food, just money; the girl was more honest.

Maybe the street sweeper man would share something of life. Then again he's busy, he doesn't even see me sitting here.

Maybe I should throw money into the parking lot. Would he see me then?

Would he at least come by as though a friend? Nah, for eventually, my money would end.

Streetlights are an odd replacement for the light of the moon. The mechanical whizzing whirr is a poor replacement for crickets.

Though I must come amongst man at times, it is then I am lonely. I deeply desire that sense of human connection; but it's not here.

At least I have recourse, a space that honors our Oneness. In nature, I feel as One. It shares all its glory; it shares its truth.

So shall I love man who shares for profit, their own gain? Who am I kidding? Is there really a difference by them and I?

My profit is my joy, my gain is sharing, I just have no price tag. So dear moon and little crickets, I'll be back, very soon.

At least in that knowing, I now feel I can sleep. Even here.

Finis

The wake of life can be cruel to love. Memories meld into our desires, then into our heart, and ravish our mind for naught in the Now. And if there is not Now, what is there? Hope? Or a Hopeless Romantic.

These days past, my heart has been calling out, and thus I write:

Where are you?

Jodie, Jodie, Jodie … Where are you Jodi

You stepped into my life so innocently
You opened your soul as though so free
You held back naught, in trust, of intimacy.

A light workers conference, we were there
Switching seats, you filled that empty chair
A Oneness Meditation, as One we did share

Sat-Chit-Ananda, we followed the call
We saw creation from the start of it all
We saw our place as to earth we did fall

We were One in that time and space, naught of remiss
But it ended not there, we owned that bliss
You and I, it sealed in our kiss

We carried it on throughout the night
The next day too, it was all so right
One more night ... then came the blight

We live afar and very different lives
Consumed by the mundane, hardly wise
Yet it is life, in those strings of such ties

Jodie, Jodie, Jodie ... Where are you Jodie

Our hearts know love that we can be
Our spirits too, there is a we
Damn the world, let's set us free

We talk of time that we might share
Yet defy the norm, do we dare
It seems to date, it's yet to bare

Desires we hold each unto our own
But time together, it is now unknown
What good is love that remains unshown

Jodie, my dear Jodie ... Where are you

By my side, I long you to be
Inside me too, for there, is we
No me no you, in that, we are free

Damn the mundane for just a while
Then in joy our hearts might smile
But being alone ... it tastes like bile

Jodie, my beloved Jodie ... Where are you

Perhaps our fate is laid by treasure
Lacking funds to endear our pleasure
Surely the rich be not held to *our* measure

To pick up and go, it seems so simple
But if it is, then what's the wrinkle
Is it a blemish, the mundane to dimple

The price of love, it disgusts my being
If by funds, it bars me you seeing
Jodie Love, do you hear my pleaing

But there's more than that, this I know
It's the daily life, our world we sow
By it then, love may never show

And when shall it be that our love prevail
That we share as One, that our grace we inhale
To think of it not … it leaves my heart to wail

Oh Jodie, my beloved Jodie … Where are you

But alas I sigh, that's of desire, what I want that be
At least there is memory, whence once it was we
Perhaps again, in another life … we'll see

A Hopeless Romantic, is that really me
I guess it's so, it's all I can see
Be well unto you dearest of Love, beloved Jodie

Finis

Life is lived in a world I suffer to embrace; and most often, so is love. Love in bits and pieces are sweet, but in the end, they hardly sate my hunger. It is my hunger to share, to share as One. It is my hunger for tomorrow that be. It is my hunger to share life.

And of the romantics, well, I guess I'm just one more; and thus I write:

Cyrano

Cyrano De Bergerac, I know your pain.
You think it's your nose, but that's just vain.
Self-worth you deigned despite your gift.
You failed your truth; you made that rift.

Am I else but you here in the end?
Reduced in love, as if but a friend.
My truth be split by life and my quest.
Mundane I'm not, and that, be loves test.

So they turn and run not to be free.
There is no room for the likes of me.
They suffer their love to life secure.
I'm left in the cold, in love obscure.

I may be loved, but what is the point?
My time alone, naught shared to anoint.
I taste of love and drink it all in.
Then I'm locked out, as if it were sin.

Don Quixote, your lesson taught me well.
That impossible dream is now my hell.
The blade of the mill turns to my reach.
I grab it yet again, naught did it teach.

But I'll go on, it is what I do.
Ever searching for the love of you.
You are out there; I know that it's true.
So yes Cyrano, I'm every bit as bad as you.

Finis

I see before me a world of qualifications and quantifications that seemingly make us real. I see it as a wrong upon man and woman alike. The worst of all, are relationships in the name of Love, and thus I write:

Vet Me?

Who be you to make me real?
Who be you to judge me?
Who be to you to sing my worth?
Who be you to see me as *your* worth?

What wrong do you seek to right
in claiming a value of me?
Or even you for that matter?

I am not here for you
nor are you here for me.
WE,
are here to share.
And nothing more.

In that, we each may grow.
I do not make you whole
nor do you make me whole.

We may share in our needs,
but neither as crutch
nor cane.

We may share our joys
but nary for lack of our own.

I shine not because of you.
I shine because I am.

Do you need witness?
A flower does not bloom for witness.
A flower blooms because it is.

I invite you to bloom,
neither for me, nor by me,
but with me.

If you cannot live by your own Truth,
how can you live with mine?
Oh,
you can't.
Silly me, vet me.

You feel judged.
We only judge ourselves.
I did hang my judge.
He vetted me.

Finis

Sometimes love springs forth when I least anticipate it. I would like to say those times are newfound women along life's journey; but that is not always the case; and thus I write:

Who are You?

I lay to sleep, or so it seems
Eyes roll back 'neath lids to dream
Purples and violets my ajna brings
And in its light such wonder springs

In pulsing glows new shapes form
I see afar, past earthly norm
Beyond the ether's open door
Energy known, Loves I adore

Spirits come and I know them too
But you're not they. Who are you?
Familiar to me in the strangest way
You show yourself, my mind at play

Are you Keaton's "la belle damn sans merci"
Your havoc you wreak, now upon me
Yet you feel so right and full of love
Your embrace like none that I think of

My head in your bosom; your chin on my crown
My heart fleshed smile; emptiness dies down
Your features seem harsh by your brilliant light
Yet your shadows lay tender as though you be wight

Essence that sparkles and fills me too
Shines in your eyes and all of you
A goddess descent might seem the case
Or am I now god and thus your embrace

And where might you be, should I look on earth
No womb of flesh would dare bring you birth
At least as I lie in my bed all alone
I know I am loved, by you it is shown

Who are you, shall I ever to know
What does it matter, I'll be your beau
Would that I find a human like you
Not apt say I, she'd be in lieu

So thank you for your blessing …
Me here …

Finis

Our love of love can drive us mad, mad with desire, mad beyond our awareness of truth, madness driven into our own hell. This I know, thus this I write:

Demonic Love

Thank you love you little daemon you. You teach us well, so very well. Well, that is presuming we are awake enough to learn. If not, like any teacher, you'll repeat the lesson.

So oft do I long for love; to share with another as One. It's that sense of connection beyond ourselves. In that great glorious moment, everything is perfect. But in that space between times of sharing, oh love, you hurt me so.

She sparks my desires in our sharing and I want more. Of course, I speak my truth and she agrees; and I fall for it, every time. Then her truth speaks louder than her words; and my heart does suffer.

My desires become my purpose for they hear not her truth; they only hear her words. They are blind; hopelessly, romantically, blind. They lead my heart, my mind, and my very being, to stumbling painfully day by day.

Promises lay in ruin and I wonder why. Yet I cling that just perhaps her words will prevail in truth. We call this co-dependency, an addiction all our own. Oh love, you daemon you.

I thank you though, for you bring pain and pain alerts us that something is wrong. Pain makes us grow. With love, there is no pain.

Finis

As a Hopeless Romantic, one has a certain problem walking through life; it is our desire, our very eagerness to share love. Like a child on the loose in a cookie jar, dare we be so open as to jump at every opportunity? Yet how dare we not? As it happened to me, thus I write:

The Chair of Fate

I see you sitting there upon your chair
A smiling face, perky, alive, how rare
Your eyes they glisten, of surprise be I
Better yet, you turn to me, and say "Hi"

I dare not to act too wanton of desire
Longing to share, bringing my heart to fire
I be seeking a spark to set me free
In your eyes and your voice, is it thee?

So I smile from my heart and say hello
But walk on by, lest my eagerness show
I had come to dance in the bonfire's blaze
For it's there I know, my prowess does raise

So I dance a bit with you on my mind
Could it be real, or like love, am I blind
I focus my eyes just to seek you out
Your energy feels clean, I've not a doubt

I'll take at least one more "O", maybe two
Then take a break and come talk with you
Pulsing drums, a fire of passion, and me
Momma's sweet earth, yet perhaps, there's we

I spin, and plant my feet to look at you
But the chair is empty, I've gone askew
By too much time, I sealed my fate
My beating heart for love does grate

I see you afar, your spirit is gone
Energy altered, it leaves me wan
You seem in a miff, frustrated at best
Did I leave you alone like all the rest?

My chance to connect, by now it is lost
Coldness abounds like the winters frost
My heart falls to earth in an endless pit
I failed my truth, to stop, talk, and sit

So blessings dear one, blew it I did
My eagerness hid neath a cast iron lid
Had I shown my heart, my true desire
I might not be left with this frozen fire

Finis

Sometimes within my bliss of life, I am blind to *all* of my truth. Other times though, it smacks me in the face, sliming my essence. Hopeless Romance can be both; flipping helplessly between the extremes.

This night, an old movie, "Single Room Unfurnished", flipped the mirror of my truth to reveal me. Thus I write:

Alone

In a world so full of people
How is it that we are so lonely
Lonely amongst one another

How is that people can not trust
Trust themselves let alone another
We can not love, if we can not trust

What is it we fear
Do we fear the loss of us
Or do we fear the loss of our dreams

Is it that if we surrender to the mundane
That our dreams were as lies
Dreams never to be, then what worth are we

Or do we fear our feelings
That feeling is pain
After all if we do not share we can not hurt

Is it that love overwhelms us
Sweeping us up, a speck of dust
We then out of control, so we think

Do strings of relationships bind us apart
A marionette entangled, unable to move
Our illusions done to us, not by us

So instead we lay, and we live, lonely
Sometimes truly alone
Sometimes lonely with another

Lonely for that glorious sense of connection
Lonely for that it is not real
Lonely, for there is only I

Lonely for we knew not we
Lonely for we saw only I
And in the end, there is no I

Finis

It would seem my ideal is to live in a field of flowers, engulfed in their majesty, drinking in their varied essence. They as love, love all around me, day by day. But oft the field is barren of flowers in bloom.

Yet before me in a land of dried, harsh grasses, did one burst forth and spread her petals. Thus of her, I must write:

Divine Space

It amazes me you come to me
So naturally, so seemingly free
You, you alone to date are the one
That really knows what had begun

There is no you there is no me
We meld to One so totally
We speak in tongues we know so well
Our voices divine much like a spell

Our bodies entwine in glorious fusion
We lose our flesh within our union
Skin we wear comes along for the ride
But the greater truth is what's inside

Our spirit essence sees we as One
We too see this, separate undone
But more than see, is to know and feel
You're there too, it makes *us* real

Our spirits entwine, we do our dance
It is of love, not just romance
I would there be more that we could share
Of life I speak, but we do not dare

Mundane for us has no place
Yet we have our sacred space
It is ours, and ours alone
That Oneness we share to the bone

Thank you Love for being so open
You answered my call, I'm no longer hopin'
Tiny bits before being almost there
Waned through time, sex in despair

The loss of self in a glorious act
To be as One in a sacred pact
More than each other, more than the whole
Synergy at work, expanding the soul

To heavens we soar beyond this earth
My spirit is blissed no longer in dearth
My mortal desires no longer have place
In divine ascent for I now know grace

Beyond the body, beyond what we feel
Our psyche revealed, illusions do peel
Our energy mounts and bursts as it may
To a heightened state wherein we do play

Therein we are whole beyond what we knew
We join with the All, not just me and you
Big bang be small in the touch of our lips
The heavens expanse is our fingertips

And when we descend to be separate beings
The bliss does remain, it's we, we are seeing
The divine in our eyes, our grace does speak
Empowered through love, we'll never be weak

So I'll rest at that and not ask for more
For what we share, is what I adore
Adulterate it not with worldly means
For as we are is that unseen

Our worlds they shift and break away
We have no place in the day to day
But it's okay, we can rise again
And share a love that need not end

Finis

Most people seem to relish my nomadic life, yet few will ever embrace it. Living as I do proves most awkward to embrace life shared together with another. Its greatest burden is that which afflicts us all in one way or another, the desire to love, to feel loved, and to share love.

There are those on occasion whom can and do share in love as it comes before them, but they are rare. There is one who embraces what we share as precious, but to meld our lives, well, thus I write:

Separate Worlds

It fascinates me how secluded we are
Our worlds we make, our freedom to bar
And then of course, how shall we share
How may we convey, that we really care

To bring each other into our life
Seems a burden filled with strife
To share as One, how shall it be
By that that we live, no room for we

Your needs are of structure, family and friends
Roots you would place where *your* road ends
For me well I roam, mostly by season
No family, no friends, a life not by reason

Inconvenient to most, my life in the Now
To share as One are questions of how
My roots they are long, that place on the map
Roads have no end, they but pause for a nap

The choices we make, important to us
Each on our own, be our personal fuss
Perhaps the best that can ever be
Is to share in that pause, a time of we

The problem is then the vanquish of hope
Hopeless I be, as though love be my dope
The end I can say for a hopeless romantic
Is to follow desire, yet be not frantic

Separate worlds we live, we choose how to be
But you share now and then, and then there is we
So thus dear one, I be bid to say, "praise you"
For shared bits of love that you give as you do

It keeps us fresh for there is no tomorrow
Withal hard on my heart, no rhyme of sorrow
While hopeless it seems, I'll live in the Now
And when we can share, the result is *Wow!*

Thank you Love

Finis

Communication, the vitality of love; it does not always need words; but sometimes, words are all we have.

Especially in times of being apart, communication can suffer unto the pace of life; life that demands and blinds us to what matters most in life; and thus I write:

Rat Race

I buy a phone that we may share
Now text and talk so debonair
Limitless voice can say I care
I carry that box now everywhere

Silence is broken; I hear the ring
I feel elated, my heart does sing
It's love from you that it does bring
Fragrance of us like buds in spring

But it's not your voice that I hear
A line of text, it says we're dear
The gift of love somehow feels queer
You, on the run, no time I hear

Feelings so deep now lain to rest
Unspoken truth now put to test
If we've no time to share our best
Then sharing love becomes a quest

And if we're not heard, what's the point
A line of text, now love disjoint
Lost expression does not anoint
Feelings deep, locked in the joint

So I write an email, words can flow
Yet what's the point, you can't read slow
Too many lines of love don't you know
Thoughts and feelings placed to show

A rat race of man, love to waste
Sweetness of love never to taste
Life in a hurry our love is baste
No time to share, our love in haste

The end of the day, energy gone
So now you call midst yawns of song
Backburner love, it feels so wrong
Too much to do, does love belong

I guess it's life, a fast-lane track
Be there room to bring love back
Or is it bundled up, a burlap sack
Hopes and dreams to lie on a rack

We use one-line texts to say it all
To worldly ways our love does fall
What once was big, now lays small
Sell the phone? Love dies in the gall

Finis

Love can begin with just a glance; it is a soulful connection seen in the eyes. A hopeless romantic will spot that look in an instant and embrace it full force. There, we lay ourselves open to all that will be. In the most mundane setting, this happened to me, and thus I write:

The Call

My guts they churn, my head it does reel,
I must tell her how I feel.
My thoughts pervade my wakened sleep,
That that is disturbs me deep.

The little things that make love grand,
It is on these that I stand.
Acceptance and truth they please me so,
It is my place to let her know.

My eyes of blue they shine, she sees my bliss,
Could anyone pass on this?
I touched her heart with just my glance,
A burning fire in new romance.

She touches my flesh and strokes my hair,
Full of affection, this maiden fair.
She speaks of me as fit, and a healthy man,
One she'd admire all she can.

Like that I am, in no other she sees,
Her heart is open, it's me she tease.
A heart so huge and she carries it well,
Could it be a witch's spell?

I buy her dinner, we sit, we chat,
She's in love, I'm sure of that.
She speaks our future that we might share,
So deep in love with no compare.

We plan a date most tentatively,
A time for us, a time to be.
We'll walk, we'll talk, we'll share in delight,
Maybe even into the night.

I place the call, and she answers with joy,
There is no point, my being coy.
"I'm breaking our date, the relationship too"
"There will be, no me and you"

Of course she asks, "What led you to this?"
"You're in your mind, blind to bliss."
"You'll change your thoughts, just give me a chance,"
"After all, it is a new romance."

"Why don't we keep our date and let us be real?"
"Then you can see how you really feel."
"I just love to joke; I'd accept that you are,"
"Don't let your mind our love to mar."

But she'd cut my hair that it be like a man,
Even my beard, my jowl now to tan.
All those places I go and the things that I do,
By her words, I should now rue.

And I do rue, she has the number to my phone,
Now she'll never leave me alone.
Caller ID, a blessing it is, her voice to gird,
Perhaps in silence my words be heard.

The cage that she painted, it glittered with gold,
But it is my truth, that she would mold.
I'm breaking our date, the relationship too,
There will be, no me and you.

Major Finis

113

Our human struggles of sharing have ravished
my being. You stand before me shaking in rivers of tears.
You sob that we are so different, it defiles your love of me;
and thus I write:

Seeing as One

When we first see one another as One,
then, we can appreciate our individuality, our uniqueness.

We are all inherently the same.
We all have the same needs.
We all have the same desires.

It is only our approach to them that is different.
It is only how they manifest, that is different.
It is only our expression of them that is different.

To see everyone the same, as One, eliminates
        separateness.
To see everyone the same, as One, eliminates the
        struggles.
To see everyone the same, as One, eliminates our fears.

It is in separateness that we fear.
It is in separateness that we lose trust.
It is in separateness that we feel alone.

To see as One, affords us a sense of connection.
To see as One, affords us self-expression.
To see as One, affords us the experience of Love.

Seeing as One acknowledges us.
Seeing as One expresses acceptance.
Seeing as One expresses appreciation.

Seeing as One is truth.
Seeing as One frees us.
Seeing as One is Love.

See me, for I see you, I see we, as One, if you let me.

To see as One does not see gender.
To see as One does not see race.
To see as One does not see ethnicity.

Seeing as One reaches beyond humanity.
Seeing as One reaches our divinity.
Seeing as One reaches the truth of Love.

See me, for I see you, I see we, as One, if you let me.

When we first see as One, then we can accept the
differences.
When we first see as One, then we can appreciate the
differences.
When we first see as One, then we can Love the
differences.

Seeing as One, we become One.
Seeing as One, we are One.
Seeing as One, we experience us as One.

See me, for I see you, I see we, as One,
if you let me.

Finis

At times in our lives, we meet very special people; and, we cannot help but feel gratitude. Our thankfulness fills our thoughts and feelings; it alters our view radiating from our eyes and often curls our lips to a smile. It becomes a major component of what love is; it is our expression of appreciation for these people.

For me it reaches beyond the mundane of life. It is the same sense I feel when seeing, smelling and touching a rose in all its wonder. It is the same sense of awe I feel watching a sunset kissing the ocean on a warm summer's eve. It is a sense of peace within me that all in the world is right, a sense that I am truly blessed.

A few years ago, I met such a woman as to inspire my sense of gratitude; I have since been afforded the chance to reconnect with her. Now, during this time, my appreciation of her has exploded. Sometimes, the only way to express our love is with a thank you; and thus I write:

Thank you Amanda

Thank you for owning the delightfully mischievous
    rascal you
Thank you for a sense of feeling at home with you
Thank you for abiding in Love as your greater truth
Thank you for accepting being "the one" despite your
    reluctance

Thank you for accepting me honoring your needs
Thank you for accepting that we love you
Thank you for actively loving me
Thank you for all that I know is yet to come, even if it
doesn't
Thank you for all the ordinary moments that become
special
Thank you for all the special moments of being you
Thank you for appreciating me
Thank you for appreciating me challenging you
Thank you for being in truth with me, no matter what
Thank you for being my morning coffee buddy when
camping
Thank you for being real
Thank you for being slender
Thank you for being so open to truth
Thank you for being spontaneous
Thank you for being strong in resolve
Thank you for being the bar of my very ideals
Thank you for being you
Thank you for calling me "Love"
Thank you for challenging me
Thank you for choosing to come back from the option
to die
Thank you for coming to me on the ether when I miss
you so
Thank you for coming to me when you are frustrated
Thank you for continuing to grow and expand your
being
Thank you for driving to see me, taking that extra effort
Thank you for embodying your pixy essence
Thank you for embracing your power

Thank you for envisioning a right land of people that
    includes me
Thank you for facilitating my needs
Thank you for feeling the energies of herbs, not just
    their names
Thank you for finding strength in me that I need not
    speak
Thank you for following your instincts instead of books
Thank you for getting past your fears
Thank you for gifting me that a relationship need not be
    work
Thank you for giving me little projects that help you
Thank you for going beyond getting it, to being it
Thank you for going into yourself even if it closes me out
Thank you for having a cute ass
Thank you for helping so many "just because"
Thank you for helping to heal me
Thank you for holding my hand as you slept
Thank you for honoring directions the Universe lies
    before you
Thank you for honoring my needs
Thank you for honoring Steve in your life
Thank you for honoring your needs
Thank you for including me amongst your special
    friends
Thank you for including me in those you love
Thank you for integrating your mind and spiritual
    awareness
Thank you for inviting me to your get-a-ways
Thank you for inviting me to your re-birthday
Thank you for keeping in touch with your soul
Thank you for knowing me
Thank you for knowing my touch as "not groping you"

Thank you for knowing that I know but being willing to
      tell me
Thank you for knowing when to bring the right people into
      your life
Thank you for knowing your soul
Thank you for knowingly coming to me in the night
Thank you for leaving the back door unlocked
Thank you for letting me be me
Thank you for letting me cook
Thank you for letting me do your laundry and fold your
      clothes
Thank you for letting me into the deepest realms of
      your truth
Thank you for letting me into your head
Thank you for letting me know your refuge if it all goes
      to hell
Thank you for letting me park my "happy ass" in your yard
Thank you for letting me participate in your hand-fasting
Thank you for letting me plug in Wicki
Thank you for letting me see you
Thank you for letting me wash the dishes
Thank you for letting the little people speak
Thank you for listening to my concerns, my joys, and
      my pains
Thank you for living your integrity
Thank you for living your truth
Thank you for long hugs
Thank you for looking me in the eye
Thank you for loving so many
Thank you for making time for me in your life
Thank you for Muah!!!
Thank you for not holding back your tears
Thank you for not making me presume

Thank you for not trying to hide your struggles too long
Thank you for our moment of dance
Thank you for reaching out with your heart and all
   your gifts
Thank you for really hearing me
Thank you for receiving shipments for me
Thank you for respecting me
Thank you for saying "I love you"
Thank you for seeing me
Thank you for sharing dinner at JB's
Thank you for sharing you
Thank you for sharing your dreams
Thank you for sharing your secret name, (even though
   I forgot it)
Thank you for sharing your snake medicine
Thank you for sharing your special place on the beach
Thank you for sharing your struggles
Thank you for sitting by the fire with me
Thank you for sitting on the doorstep with me
Thank you for speaking and sharing your truth
Thank you for standing up for your truth and yourself
Thank you for standing up to the challenges of being
   Mom
Thank you for surrendering your resistances
Thank you for taking charge of what you need to
   and when
Thank you for taking refuge in Wicki
Thank you for that stern stance when you're angry
Thank you for the boldness with which you march forth
   in life
Thank you for the crunched wrinkles between your eyes
Thank you for the guts to be "different"
Thank you for the hugs

Thank you for the long talks, even about others
Thank you for the smile from your heart, through your eyes
Thank you for the smile on my face and heart in
      thoughts of you
Thank you for the sparkle in your eye
Thank you for the two beautiful beings you brought into
      the world
Thank you for thinking of me to go rescue Barbie
Thank you for understanding healing
Thank you for understanding my snake dream
Thank you for waking me at ungodly hours simply
      by connection
Thank you for watching the sunrise with me
Thank you for wearing cute underwear
Thank you for wearing your balls on your chest
Thank you for your clarity of truth
Thank you for your kiss
Thank you for your laugh
Thank you for your openness in sharing love
Thank you for your shameless nakedness
Thank you for your solid presence in your body
Thank you for your thoughts of me
Thank you for your touch
Thank you that I can cry a tear by the wrench of your
      heart
Thank you that I can feel your presence anywhere,
      anytime
Thank you that I see me in the mirror of you
Thank you that my cheeks hurt from smiling with you
Thank you that my name spills from your lips as part of
      your life
Thank you that our sharing is not about life's little
      dramas

Thank you that our sharing is not about times past but
    of Now
Thank you that we can be at peace in times of silence
Thank you that this list seems un-endable and
    incomplete

Finis

At times, words pale what truth I speak; yet at times, those words are precious and need to flow forth; and thus I write:

Amazing

What we share amazes me
Our sense of One that we be
Time and space comes and goes
But when we join it never shows

Early on I saw One, not two
Reflections of me I see in you
It feels so natural in space we share
As if to say there is we. And I dare

Our lives seldom cross and mix
Varied roads, they are our twixt
Hardly a call, a text, or mail
But what we share does not fail

In times as you hunker down, I pain
A world on your ass, I feel your strain
Then I feel you raise up your shield
By your strength there is naught to yield

I would reach out and aid your quest
But I honor your truth and lie to rest
And when you pop up, I see your joy
The beauty of you, naught could destroy

You withdraw from me only as you need
And when you are done, our love you feed
Your very presence and all that you are
You share in your truth, nothing to bar

I laugh when I hear what people say
They see us partnered all the way
I've yet to know why it is never so
But it doesn't matter, we share the glow

A list of thanks speaks so little
Expressions of love that I whittle
We amaze me Amanda and always will
The beauty of us, must flow my quill

Finis

Hear me

By the power vested in me as the Hopeless Romantic
In Poetic Voice I do now proclaim
That you, Amanda
Are now and forever more
One of my greatest experiences in Love

Thus I inscribe your name as your essence
for all eternity
That as the Gods look upon thee
They too shall smile, as do I

So it is said
So it is written
So it is done

Sometimes we are inspired by the greatest of love; love that is pure; love that is free and true. To my delight, I have shared such love and in honor of that, to her I did write:

Josalynn

Blessings there my dearest of love, you've answered my quest as from above. Nothing held back by your spirit here, your essence in full and all so pure.

You've come forth as my very ideal, answering true my hearts appeal. You embody truth beyond mortal man, I'll share all you want, I'll share all you can.

Your eye's they sparkle like stars so near, yet too is the vastness of through which you peer. They lock with mine as you see into me, a gifted trust of your purity.

Within your gaze, I feel real; accepted as me, it is honored I feel. To see me in truth is all that I've asked; my bliss by your gaze, for there I have basked.

But you see more than me, of all that could be, you see truth, our eternity. Into the heavens, our home you stare; yet in nature here, your Oneness is rare.

Your kiss, it is gentle though backed by passion; the best of all, it comes without ration. Your lips they are sweet for they speak of your being, speaking too of all that you're seeing.

Your skin it is soft, a delight to touch; your embrace it is real, I long it so much. Beyond your flesh, your essence you share, energy flowing, no boundaries you dare.

Your smile, your joys, your passions, your pain, there's nothing you hide, nothing you feign. You share it all, the beauty of you; my hungry heart fed, leaves nothing to rue.

You bring me gifts, your world to share, your treasures of life, laid to bare. There's nothing you'd keep to hold to your own, you lavish my being, to your very bone.

I'm humbled in awe by your love for me, given so freely,
simplistically. How shall I share? What have I to give?
It confuses my mind this life we live.

Three days we had, I'll not ask for more; by love you have
shared; your truth I adore. No woman I know could fill that
space; I'd rather be alone in the human race.

Thank you Love for touching me, for being you, for being
free. You struck me deep your power of levin, but
the madness of all, your earthly years seven.

Finis

One of our primary needs as humans is a sense of connection. For many it can manifest in our desire to find our soul mate; that special someone whom we loved so dearly. In ways, I'm no different; but there
is a twist; and thus I write:

The Old Soul Blues

There are we who have walked this plane, this planet, for a very long time. We have had multitudes of shared lives, oft with loves of ere. Yet others were loves in the bud with promise of bloom.

We see them now and then. It suffers us like lost at sea whence recognition occurs liken ships in passing.

Suffer say I? Verily. In space of naught, a wanton heart, expression of love wide asunder, charged in vain to nary an opposing pole, yea, of this it suffers.

Ageless memory stirs reborn. Sweetness of flesh fills my nares. Salivations whet my lips in desire. Without repress mine soul doth leap. I fall through you to dance as One. But then the Now, the damnable Now.

Mine eyes behold, Oneness retold.
But harken the Now, sojourn we not in days of old.
Of you and we, before me here are very different lives.

Lives besieged. Be it age, direction of life in hand, the
need to fulfill our soul's work in this time, they all lay claim.

Aged soul be still. To mortal life you have died countless
times. This is just one more passing. But within lay the
abyss heart.

Nay expression, might of heart lumens pale.
Parting yet again serves a breathless ankh,
and death within.

Finis

At a time in my life, I had the pleasure of a dearest of love travel with me extensively about the country. Needless to say, the five weeks were all too short a time; but something miraculous happened.

She rocked my world; she disheveled it, and turned it upside down; all in the pure innocence of her being. Even her clothes for the hour oft lie spewed about; nothing was normal; but rather, it was exciting. And yet, she continuously thanks me for helping her; thus, I write:

Who helped Whom?

You needed space to be yourself,
To find your truth above all else.
At my pleasure you came to me,
To know yourself and be free.

In helping you, you truly helped me,
You opened my eyes, *my* truth to see.
You caused me to look at my own space,
And how I mix in the human race.

Ideals I held, and things I liked,
Desires to be, by you they spiked.
To be myself in great extremes,
You freed my mind to live *my* dreams.

Conservative and bland is now no more,
To such thoughts, I've closed the door.
I've stretched my norms for clothes I wear,
They speak of me, I'm free to dare.

My seating, my linens, they all have changed,
In poverty no more, it's all rearranged.
The way I bathe and the food I eat
They're different now and kind of neat

It was all in my mind that world I knew,
I changed it all through helping you.
I'm far more free in expressing me,
I put myself forth for all to see.

I now feel entitled, worthy and free,
You led me to break *my* shackles of me
Though I be headed there long and slow,
In helping you my spark blew to glow.

I breathe in life and all it can be,
My being and spirit do now agree.
You rocked my world and set me free,
Thank you so much for helping me.

Finis

In the stillness of night, beyond clatter of light, comes truth; comes knowing. Revelations descend past mental obstructions and take form. It is in this space, this time, that everything becomes clear.

Then, as we attempt to abstract it all back through the mind, we are bombarded by mass consciousness; thoughts that speak we are mad. But are we? I say nay. I have heard; I have seen; and thus I write:

The Knowing

What is going on
Why this madness
My desires run rampant
I lie awake
I want
I want in the Now

The voices
They talk to me
I know beyond knowing
I see the power of love
Its truth
It's sharing as One
I know it

Our very lives
Our existence
It is not in balance with what is
It is not in balance with truth
Love is truth
And by love
By sharing as One
It is by that
And that alone
That we live long
We thrive
We grow beyond singularity
We rejuvenate
We expand

It is by the lack of we that the I dies
The I is eternal in we
For the I does not exist there
My desire then
My desire then is to share
To be as One
How can we not
Why would we not

We are not designed to live short
To die early
To be of ill
To bear disease
To be malformed
To be alone

This the Universe speaks to me
This truth
This knowing

We are supplied with desire
As is the All
Desire, the potential
The All
Love is the All
Love is sharing
Love is the expression of the All
I hear you
I know you
I will abide
How can I not

Am I mad
Insane
It doesn't matter
For I know what is real
I know what is true
And by that I live eternal
By that, I live long even in the flesh

And with whom shall I share
All who also hear the voices
All who also know of truth
All who also know of love
All who also live of love
How can we not

Desire
How can we deny what is real
How can we live the mundane
How can we live without desire
We cannot
We die
We rot
We cease

And so then
Will you share with me
Will you be as One with me
Will you embrace truth
Will you embrace love
Or must we die

Desire unmet pains
Pain speaks of death
For love knows not pain
There is no pain in love
There is only pain in desire unmet
There is only death in desire unmet

And to whom do I speak
Only those who hear
Only those who know
Only those who feel the fire
The fire of desire

I already know you
You know me
For we are already One
All we need do is embrace
Make that leap
Let go and enjoin
Embrace love

What more is there
Nothing
Nothing at all
Not even the void

So why not in the Now
Why by some plan
A plan of the mind
A harness of the heart
A shackle of desire
A crypt for love

And by whom shall love die
By whom shall love be denied
And you call me mad
You call me insane

I hear you
The voices
The knowing
There must be others
It cannot only be my ears
I am no different
It is only that I listen
I see
I know
And if we are here
Then where are *we*
How shall others see if we do not embrace
How shall others hear if we do not share
How shall other ever know
How shall others ever love

To write it on paper as some tribute
It is hollow
Scribbles of nothing
Ideals unmet
Desire only described
Desire never lived
Desire that died

If you're out there
Somewhere
Hear my voice
See me
Know me
Embrace me
For that is love
That is I
That is *we*

Therein we can live long
Live well
Live life
Live love
Live sharing
There is nothing more

Hear me lest my voice go mute
See me lest I cease
Lest I pass for desire unmet
Lest I die for love unshared

Hear me
See me
Love me
And share with me

Finis

Love has come before in bits and pieces;
sometimes, but rarely, it has dwelt awhile. But in this
time, there is a unique difference of which I must write:

Your Love of Me

You bless my being, your love of me
Your healing touch, embodied divine
You act as compeer, you see my truth
In energy raised, it is energy shared

You bless my being, your love of me
Aft years of desire my passions embraced
Orgasms abound though nary a climax
I feel accepted, appreciated, alive and real

You bless my being, your love of me
Words of thanks pale of its greater truth
Even feeling you afar, my tracks they stop
I lose myself, it is shared with you

You *all* bless my being, your love of me
And there are more, but not in this moment
Feeling so loved, all at once
Everywhere I turn, you bless my being

I've walked this land unloved so long
Now it flows like water drenching my soul
Magical beings, you have come to me
You bless my being, your love of me

Finis

We all want to experience Love. Sometimes, love appears most unexpectedly. And in those all too rare moments, we may find the most important love of all. It happened to me with such great force, that I must write:

I see you Love

You were right before me all this time
It is as though I've been so blind

You groomed yourself to great appeal
Done all those things that make you real

You took time and space to be at your best
And blessed yourself with time for rest

You chose your clothes with great attention
You look your sharpest beyond all mention

That rose quartz heart draped with care
You wear your truth on bosom bare

The glint of your eyes has sparked anew
They show the love inside of you

You smile and wink, then blow me a kiss
Whispers of "I love you" then bring me bliss

You trimmed your hair just for me
Looking oh so sexy, like I love to see

Thus, I stand and look at you
And wonder how I ere felt blue

How grand it is you have come to me
Thank you Love, for it is *you* I see

It's hard to fathom you are really here
But there I am, in my own mirror

Finis

What can I say …

of Lady N

Though Lady N had an impact on previous poems you've read thus far, the rest of this book evolved by my love of her. They are presented in the order as written by date of transcription. As is my habit when writing of someone, these were sent to Lady N; well, most of them were ... the writings shall speak their truth, my voice, as The Hopeless Romantic.

Lady N

It's rather uncommon to meet exceptional spiritually connected people as anything more than passing ships in the fog; yet on occasion they do more than just blink their lights. And sometimes, just sometimes, we meet and really connect.

It's seldom a matter of reuniting souls; it's more a matter of recognition of one another in truth of our essence. I have been blessed by such a being, and thus I write:

Meeting Lady N on the Ether

Thank you so much for coming to me
In the ether, there is a we
I'm not alone, it's not just me
It's our place, where we, become free

I've watched you oft these years of past
You made an impression sure to last
With your smile, your spell you cast
A place in my heart, has long held fast

Others have seen my interest in you
They cursed your beauty through and through
They, dwelling in fear, it's nothing new
They feared their loss in my love for you

Silly they, they knew not love
The very essence you are of
Divine descension from above
I love not just you, rather you as love

Of course through time they've all gone away
For its only true love that's destine to stay
But that's okay, each gave what they may
We've shared through it all for love is our way

Moksha we share to the highest degree
That state of union, as One are we
We've shared of bliss and pains that be
We've embraced each other in a loving spree

But now on the ether, you've open the door
You come to me, offering more
I laugh when I ask, why not before
To love on this plane, I do so adore

The ether is real, every bit as are we
For in that space, we're completely free
Free from the mundane that upon us be
Free to share in divine reality

For that is us, it is as we are
This flesh we wear only goes so far
As spirit essence, we are on par
Sharing our souls, there's nothing to bar

To heal and to nurture, it's all such a joy
Using our gifts, our love to deploy
We can share it all, no need to be coy
We've always been real, for love's not a toy

Even there, I see your smile
The light of your eyes, an eternal mile
Like walking on earth, your presence does while
It acts like a magnet, a mystical wile.

But then on earth, that's precious too
If closer could be, I yearn closer to you
To manifest our truth, I would to do
To share it all, that is my woo

And perhaps yet someday, it shall come
That you and I, closer as One
Bringing to whole what has begun
Some space and time, ours, bar none

In the mundane, our lives disagree
There's not much hope of sharing in we
But it's okay, that is not my dream to be
My dream is of space, for a you and me

And if those limits, by whom we each are
Bar my joy, and keep us afar
We have a place where we are on par
The ether my love, we shine like a star

So thank you Lady N, for all that you give,
and meeting me on the ether.

Sametha

Finis

The attributes of a woman can be special; they can be amazingly special. One of my greatest loves has such an attribute; and to her I write:

Your Smile

You smile
And I melt
I am at awe
I must smile too

You may not even be smiling at me
But whether you are or not
My spirit comes alive

Your smile
Were it but painted lips
It would betoken little
But it is not

You smile from your heart
It pours through your eyes
It shines through your skin
It trickles over your being
It curls your lips
It expresses your soul

Your smile
It is you at peace
It is you in balance
It is you as divine
It is you as love
It is you, as you are

Sometimes
Sometimes I see it first in you energy
The way you walk
The way you look
Your very presence

Sometimes
Sometimes I see it first on your face
The curl of your lips
The glow that sets you apart
The warmth of your being

Sometimes
Sometimes I see it first in your eyes
Even when not looking at me
That is what makes it so beautiful
You smile for you
Because you are you

Your smile
It is like a rose that blooms
It is beautiful
It simply blooms because it is
Your smile opens like the rose
Because it is
Because it is you

And when you smile at me
My spirit joys
It joys because I am seen
Seen through your smile
The smile by your eyes
You share it with me
You include me

Your smile
Mona Lisa yields as pale
She is bland
She is boring
She is lifeless

But you
Your smile
It is divine
It is your heart
It is your spirit
It is your love expressed

Thank you for wearing your smile
Thank you for owning your smile
Thank you for being your smile

It is genuine
You are genuine
It is your truth
Of your heart
Of your love
Of your being

It radiates
It frees
It enlivens

It is your heart
How you see
How you are

It spills forth like water
It rises forth like fire
It whispers like gentle wind
It fleshes like mother earth
It shines like immortal spirit

Thank you
Thank you for your smile

Finis

Sometimes in life, we are lucky, lucky enough to dwell in love. There is a beauty to it being but sometimes lest we be consumed, even obsessed. Of course, one might expect nothing less from a Hopeless Romantic.

Yet we must be real. Is there a flower eternally in bloom? Is there a sunset that never kisses the horizon goodbye? Is there a grand symphony that has no ending? Is there icing for a cake that has no cake? Shall our passions and joys of life all lie upon someone else?

Of course, sometimes we want more; but sometimes, sometimes is perfect, and thus with reverence I write:

Sometimes

Sometimes you are the sun that peeks through a
     cloudy day
Sometimes you are the fading sunset in promise of
     a bright tomorrow

Sometimes you are the sparkling dewdrop in the
     morning mist
Sometimes you are a raging river of passion that
     sweeps me away

Sometimes you are present when I most need nourished
Sometimes you are the warmth that wraps me on chilly
    nights

Sometimes you are the moon glow that lights my way
Sometimes you are the moon in its darkness with only
    my trust in knowing that you are there

Sometimes you are the sexual energy that swells
    within me
Sometimes you are the release that crumples my legs
    like rubber

Sometimes you are the smile I can't help but smile
Sometimes you are the smile smiling back at me

Sometimes you are a memory, a desire, and a joy
    all at once
Sometimes you are with me but a heartbeat, but it
    feels eternal

Sometimes you are a vast state of peace in which
    I float
Sometimes you are the adrenaline rush that bursts
    in my heart

Sometimes you are wordless, silent whispers
    of knowing
Sometimes you are the ears I endlessly jabber at
    like a child

Sometimes you are the inspiration to lay awake at night
Sometimes you are the madness by which I crawl out of
    bed to write such folly

Sometimes it nice to be me and feel so loved
Thank you Lady N. These ethereal visions of you
blessed me. I knew them as you, you in greater truth to
the vastness of your Divine Essence; they are you as you
came before me.

Finis

To share in love, yes, it can consume our thoughts, our drive, even our ability to express much else. It changes our appreciation of life.

And then along comes Lady N. She brings it all to my plate. I'm not even sure I can write; but in this space, these words come forth:

Scattered and Stuck

Scattered?
Whom am I kidding?
You've broken my norms
I fall into "stuck"

Stuck like now
What can I possibly write that serves what we share?
That serves "us"
Words, they pale

Yes, you glow
I laugh
So do I
Inside out

Stuck
Stuck and scattered

And how can I leave?
How can I drive away from this?
How can I let the sunset?
I know it is inevitable
Or is it?

We create our reality
Our truth
Our Now

Your name is filling my inbox
I cannot delete them
They are windows to you
I laugh
I scoff
Windows?
Dare I say I want more?
Dare I say I want the flesh too?

The smile
The energy
The depth of your eyes
Dare I say I want it all?

Broken platters
Melted bowls
Cupboards we dare not open
Dare I say I want it all?

I did dare
You answered affirmatively
You embraced me
You embraced my flesh
You embraced my spirit
You embraced my soul
You embraced me whole
I still hear you Buddha
You're laughing
Attachment
Attachment

I'm laughing too
But Buddha, I have held the Holy Grail of Love
I have touched it to my lips
I have spilled its essence into my being
And it nourishes me
Deeply

The Grail
It is you Lady N
I write your name
I am stuck
I am scattered
I lose focus
Well
On anything but you

381 years have passed
Years never feeling loved
She finally came and led me to break my curse
But she could not fulfill my desire to love in the Now
It is not where she needs to be

Love had set me free
Finally

Desire
I dared speak it
You chose to embrace it

I sit scattered in thought
Stuck
What direction am I to be led?
Is this why I was told to stay south for the summer?
Is this the "something big" I have felt coming?

And as I drive away
Ouch
Words to suffer

I can't keep my train of thought
I can't even find the tracks
There are rails and ties running random
The engine is primed
Steamed
Ready to roll

Roll where?
Oh my
If it were but a short jaunt, it would be fine
But more than two months
Really?
Must I?
And by who's command?

NRE?
New relationship energy?
Bull
I laugh
I've been there by others
I've seen it
But it need not be real

Again I laugh
So do I drive away to keep NRE alive?
Man
That sucks
I'd rather live it
Experience it
Dwell in it
Roll and play and rest in it
Let that Grail pour over me
Through me
Beyond me

And you
You Lady N
You do it
I may seem scattered
I may seem stuck

Okay
Seem?
I am

You are the first I've found to share on my level
The first to really "get it"
Experience it
Be it
Share it

There may be others
Others I've yet to find
But I've been looking a long time
Maybe I wasn't ready
Maybe I needed to break that curse
Nah, it's not just that
I saw you and loved you before it was broken
I desired all along to share
To share in you
To share with you

And we did
Well
Within "limits"
And now I laugh
There are still limits
Even some by the fears of others
But I trust
I trust those other limits to be gone in time
I'll try to resist commanding it
Maybe

Well, maybe not
The Universe loves me
It listens to me
Yeah, okay
I shall be aware of my thoughts
Thoughts not to command
But rather accept

I want to share with you
You, Lady N
Stuck
Scattered
Your smile
Your eyes
Your energy
Your love
Your nurturing
Your very essence
Your acceptance
Your appreciation
Your embrace
You, as Divine Essence

It is as I've seen you
As I've known you
As I've desired
And now
Now it's real
Real for me
For me to drink in
Yeah, okay
Am I just a spoiled little brat?
Am I just starved for love?

Am I just a Hopeless Romantic?
Am I just insane?
Am I scaring you away yet?

Hours of work I had to do
Well
It all still needs done
Go ahead
Scatter me
Leave me stuck

So sometimes, sometimes is perfect?
To a point
Maybe if
But that was sometimes in such diversity
All those little things
The little things that make loving you so grand

So go ahead Lady N
Scatter me
Leave me stuck
And know my gratitude

me here ...

Finis

What fool coined parting as sweet sorrow? Sure,
if I do not experience love in the highest degree, how can
I know the depth of its absence? Oh my, drinking from the
Holy Grail of Love has left its mark. So too now has the
aftermath; and thus I write:

Just a Little Lost

I awake this morn in confusion
You had not visited me during the night
You had been where you needed to be
That is as it should be

It is not that you come every night
Perhaps it is more that I felt your absence
I hesitate to come to you, to be invasive
That too is as it should be

Yet I felt little bits of you all around me
I looked for you sitting on the cushion
But you have faded, now nearly invisible
That too is as it should be

But I am confused
Nothing looks right
I open my door
Eventually the cement looks right

I feel lost
Where am I?
You felt me withdraw myself when leaving
Did I leave too much of me behind?

I finally make the long morning walk
My third night here
And I have trouble finding the restroom
It too does not look right; it is not the same

Am I finally feeling overwhelmed
In a land lain out like a maze?
A maze full of mice going nowhere
A maze that has no entrance, and no exit

And the mice, most are blind
Some squint at me at best
I do not belong here
But I do not know where here is

I think I know where I am going
But I do not really know why
I feel lost
Thank heaven for Garmin

I go to buy food, even a green pepper
I like green peppers
I put it in a little bag, then in my cart
I go around the corner to buy an onion

I turn around and an imp has taken my pepper
He put another pepper there instead
And without a bag
It was not nearly as nice a pepper

I go through the long line and pay the piper
Unloading my bags, I realize something
I forgot a bag
At least the cashier still had it for me

I am still lost though
Lost and tired, very tired
I have struggled all morning
I feel numb

Am I numb from uncertainty?
The effect of walking away from love
Is it just my fear that there is no tomorrow?
I have suffered myself for that before

I laugh; tomorrow
Tomorrow only exists when I get there
I cannot live in tomorrow
But today, I am numb

But you have plans
My thoughts perk
It is not just all me
Plans, those hopes we dream to come

To hope though disempowers everyone
It leaves expectations upon you
Dependency by me for naught of self-direction
Hopes are simply desire without direction or life

I cannot do that to you
I cannot do that to me
Well, maybe just a little bit is okay
Yes, I hear me Buddha, go ahead and laugh

You will need a place to sleep
I will wash the sheets
You say you will like that
Dare I say I have done it for some time now, just in case?

But then, do you want the natural linen
Or do you prefer satin
I cannot yet find silk sheets to my liking
I guess we can figure it out

And gee, then there are the pillows
I have two buckwheat hull pillows in use
But I also still have my down pillows
Maybe you will want your own pillow

Just a little bit huh?
Is that why I am so very tired?
So very numb
So very lost

I cannot stand it any more
I lay down to sleep
Two long hours later and I awaken
At least now, I can see you

Those bits of you I felt before
They sparkle now like little orbs
The orbs fairies wear coming to me from out
        of the woods
But they feel like you; is there a difference?

So I surrender to Now and drive south
I need music so I pull out an Abba CD
They have always touched something inside me
I cry at nearly every verse, feelings I had to let go

I have no idea what they were; they just had to go
At least by midafternoon, I begin to come back
        into myself
My newly potted flowers are smiling at me
I think they are growing too

Tomorrow ... in the beginning,
Waiting for tomorrow was a year long
Then it changed to scheduled gatherings
Now, now tomorrow cries that it is not today

Times suffered before,
They were my desires of what could be
But this, this is my desire of what is
And dare I say it is not *only* me

I made the trip, a scant 115 miles
I am exhausted
Again I lay to sleep
This time, waking finds me a little more together

When deciding to shower
I realize I have left the hot water tank on
It wastes propane; it wastes water
I have to play around now so it does not burn me

I can only question what am I doing?
Dinner, oh yes, food, I have not been very hungry
Even last night my appetite for food was low
Tonight, it seems even worse

Why did I buy my pepper in the morning?
It was to be food for the gathering
And that does not start until tomorrow, oh yeah,
Tomorrow, and a wasted day in the short life of a pepper

I buy a small serving of macaroni salad
Even it was too much and left me queasy
I also bought a small fruitcake
I like fruitcake, but I could not eat it

Maybe my stomach was preparing for this
Maybe I just knew it was coming
After all, the sun had to set
Whom am I fooling but me?

And what makes me think I can drive off again
A world of tomorrows and plans
Gatherings of desire lie many miles away
It may be a very long summer

Summer gatherings always seemed short
Now they dwell in the land of forever
Worse yet, they are my choices, my desires
Conflict, conflict causes tension, no wonder I am tired

No wonder I am lost
The weights of desires are imbalanced
The waters currents are thrashing hard
I have lost my bearings

I guess all I can do is trust
Trust the Universe, and trust you
I laugh; I must trust me before I trust you
That is hard right now, I am just a little lost

My eyes swell moist in that, even still
It is all okay though, I guess so anyway
Trust, surrender, and accept the Now
Accept what is, for that is the truth of the Now

I had waited long to share with you
You finally opened the door and invited me in
I cannot ask for more than that, well, maybe not
I guess we will figure it out, maybe tomorrow

Thank you making what room on your plate you did
You have blessed me
Even if I end up going through this all over again
I will do it again, just to be on your plate

Thank you Lady N

Finis

The next morning, I awoke feeling fine. Feeling fine, but still full of desire, and with a smile from my heart.

Lady N

175

Sometimes just one little comment can reel my mind. Though most people would not have taken his comment personally, his statement struck me deeply. It took considerable time to unravel its impact upon me. Through the course of understanding myself, I am led to write:

My Muse?

These works I write are simple but true
They seem to speak mostly of you
And truth be known you share their power
You call through my vision in many an hour

One did say you be my muse
But to call you such, rends abuse
My muse is my soul, my spirit, my heart
They form the words I do impart

I cannot speak what I do not see
I speak the love you share with me
Our essence divine takes many forms
Separate not, despite all the norms

I cannot speak what I do not feel
I speak the love that by you is real
Love is shared with another as One
In this space, be my heart undone

176

And if I reduce you to label by name
I'd separate us, thus love in defame
I'll label you not, no more than myself
For those are ideals to sit on a shelf

I cherish your expression, the very you
Alive and changing, growing anew
But you've grown inside me, and changed me too
My soul, my spirit, my heart beyond what they knew

So as my words come forth, they are different now
For I am no longer the I, I as some sacred cow
You have entered my id at my very source
All that I am, does thus change, but of course

I'll not diminish the gifts you bring
I'll not deny how my heart wants to sing
But there is only one thing I'll label you of
You are one of my greatest experiences of Love

Thank you Lady N

Finis

At times, my written works are simply my way of resolution to that which I cannot understand before their inscription. Typically, by the end of its writing, I am resolved. But that word was "typically".

Shiva Lingam

How do I keep my balance? Balance between love of you and love of life; love of the world around me. The stone calls to me; so I invite the vender to fashion a hemp necklace to my liking. It now hangs about my neck. Can I set the heart-shaped rose-quartz pendant aside for now? It has held place for me; worn all but when showering. But now, I need balance. Or is that true?

How can I have balance if I remove my heart; albeit that was only a pendant; it was still what I needed then. It is not that my heart lacks presence without you in the flesh. My heart simply desires to share presence with you; for that is love in the manifest. What serves love if it is not shared? Nothing, nothing but memories. I laugh; memories that smile within my heart and upon my face.

How can I dwell in peace if I am unbalanced? Peace is being in balance. To experience you is to experience peace, and yes, even the memory finds peace; but it is peace residing in memories of yester-days. Feelings and experiences held as memory turn into emotions; they trap us into the past. I cannot live in the past. I must live in the Now.

How can I embrace the emptiness of Now against the desire of sharing with you? It rends me of warmth liken standing naked to a blizzard. It finds me frozen as chiseled in stone by the Medusan gaze; the very gaze of mine eyes into me. Must I then search out the fire of new passion in a relentless quest? Then it becomes a matter of focus, but on which, desire, or Now? Shall I focus upon the Now with my eyes and heart wide open? It is as I would this walking soul to be. But must I condemn me to focus that I am able to leave you in the past, and be in the Now? I cannot; that serves as but surrogate love; I will dishonor neither of us with that.

How shall I embrace life in its ongoing flow? Three short months ago, I dreamt naught to mix in the mundane of you. My dreams now are a wakened state; wakened to the greater beauty and fullness of sharing with you. Even the simple amoeba swims to that which nurtures its essence. How can I be anything less than he?

How can I honor my fleshed essence amidst a world fearful of its greater truth? A crow came this morning to talk to me. He came closer than most humans ever will. His caw spoke of his truth; he shared it with me. Truth, there is no love without truth. There is no love in fear. If my skinned essence shall rival an amoeba, I must swim to truth, to love, to trust. I must swim to that which nourishes me.

How do I find my balance in desire as to abate an overload, an overload upon you? Do I simply dwell in too many moments without focus? Nay, I am focused, focused on that which honors that I am; focused on truth, love, and trust. Yet we must be real? What hopeless idiot dared say that? Sometimes *is* perfect, sometimes.

How do I honor the expression of me, that that I am, if not by the likes of you? You be too few, too scattered. Those that come close can only do so for but a moment; they dwell in their fears. I desire more; I desire my daily manna untainted; I would rather starve. Is my starvation then the emptiness of the Now, the Now that reeks of obsession? Am I, like the humans, now embracing fear?

How can I fear? If I fear, I cannot love, and thus I fail my own truth. If I fear, then I am not in trust, and thus I fail my own truth.

How do I find my balance? I do not know. Brother crow he speaks of wisdom, so too Shiva Lingam, marked in balance of wisdom. I have partaken of the Grail, what more can I ask? Is it then time for me to transcend the flesh and leave it behind? I have only just begun to appreciate it. Does the caterpillar resent leaving behind its found glories of life while cocooned in the emptiness of Now? If I can be the amoeba, can I not be the caterpillar?

How do I find my balance? I do not know, perhaps, only by knowing imbalance. Thank you Lady N for inciting transformation, I trust my dinning confusion shall not overwhelm.

Finis

Through years of experience in relationships, it has always amused me that I might miss the little things of importance to a partner. Little things like a new color of nail polish; even worse is missing those new shoes to match her dress. Heaven forbid it be something as big as that hair trim.

Love though, may lead us to blindness on other levels leaving our face a tad flush. But going deeper yet, our embarrassment can bring us to our knees as we struggle to resolve our truth; and thus I write:

Embarrassed to Humility

At times, I must own my embarrassment
I miss gifts of vision my eyes are lent
Tattoos you wear are laying there
I saw them not on your skin so bare

Your bosom too, I missed how endowed
A very asset makes some women proud
Your portrait in profile I missed by a mile
It showed naught your eyes nor your smile

But there is one worse, worse by far
I am embarrassed for, the Love you are
A Hopeless Romantic, a knower of Love
No candle I hold by that you are of

People claim that I am loving and kind
But as they speak I think they be blind
They see me not as a being in whole
They miss both sides, this walking soul

It's not that I'm angry, brazen or crude
I seldom have reason to be very rude
Yet when I look at love and know its truth
You exceed me by far, your being, so sooth

You accept more than I, or at least so it seems
More than I would claim in my wildest dreams
To accept without condition, that is loves way
Yet beings of ill, I keep them at bay

It's not I need judge nor part condemnation
They're simply not given, my contemplation
Severity and mercy, each in one hand
The middle pillar, in balance I stand

I let the chips fall, each as they may
It is what I do; it's the roll I obey
Sometimes it is hard, the pains that I see
But I stay them back lest they suffer me

But I look at you, your arms open wide
You'd save them all with nothing to hide
You accept as they come, it is the beauty of you
Yet you walk away clean, to yourself you are true

Humanity might fall but the likes of you
Love you impart, you give through and through
Though I smile at your gift, humbler I be
For I cannot match you, it's not within me

I will not blame me, nor diminish my being
But when I think of Love, it is you I am seeing
Then I laugh, we see in others a mirror of us
So am I seeing me, in you, and why should I fuss?

I'll not place you on some pedestal throne
Me looking up, you there, all alone
That pedestal throne is seating for two
Compeers of Love, both me, and you

Though seated aside and glowing as one
I feel humble, for alone, you outglow the sun
So grateful am I, that you choose me too
Your gift of Love, the sharing of you

Thank you Lady N for humility, humility and Love

Finis

Sometimes our desires are simple, yet profound.
Having a desire fulfilled can only lead me to write:

Wow

What a treasure, what a gift
To sleep beside you
To be in trust of space shared so intimately,
   so openly, so lovingly, thank you

I know it was a rare long shot of my dreams
Dreams of what may be
But at least in this time it was real
Wow, there is magic in dreams that come true
I thank the gods for cold weather
I thank the gods for convenience of space
I thank the gods for your love of me
I thank you for sharing your love

Of course I lay awake the first hour or more
How could I not?
Just the joy of watching you
To watch you release the tensions of the day
To watch you fall comfortably into sleep
To watch you sleep in peace
To watch you breathe

After all, for me it was like being a little kid
    on the night before Christmas
Santa Clause really came down that chimney
Better yet, he brought me exactly what I'd dreamt of
You, sleeping beside me in the flesh
Oh, don't get me wrong, nights you come on the ether,
    they are precious to me too
But wow, this was humanly real, humanly alive, a gift,
    a treasure

I'd dreamt of folding around you and you around me
We did
It was real
It was natural
It felt so right, so perfect, so exactly as I'd dreamt of,
    hoped for, longed for

You could have pitched that tent
After all, you don't mind being alone
And having time and space alone is important
But you didn't make that choice, it was a choice, you chose
    to share of time and space, you chose to share the gift
    of you, your presence, your loving essence
And you made that choice to share it with me

Wow

Oh, I know, two people in love can share that space in
the beginning and have it fall away into complacency
And after all, the second night I didn't lay awake so
terribly long
It was more as if I could really just let it be
Let myself acknowledge that it is real and accept
the glory, the gift, the treasure
I awoke the first morning and you were still there
It was not a dream
Your eyes met mine with a smile
It was beautiful
I could just be me, and feel loved

Wow

Thank you Lady N
It may not have meant to you what it meant to me
And if not, that is okay
It can be my own little glory of the moment
After all, I am a Hopeless Romantic
Isn't that what we do?
Live for all those little treasures we find along the way
Well, at least I still have the dream that it may come again
And better yet than a dream, it really happened
Thank you Lady N

Finis

Then of course, there are the nights that follow
Nights like tonight
Nights when I wake up and lay there counting cycles
of the furnace

It is nights like these that sometimes you have been
    there on the ether and wrapped around me just as you
    did in the flesh
But tonight is not one of them

I can still feel you there though, there in my bed,
    there beside me
You left your sparkling energy en masse
Silly you, didn't you catch that part of the workshop
    on cleaning up your energy footprint
I smile
I'm glad you didn't do it
(Or was that deliberate?)
In fact, I can feel your energy all around me
So now, it is like waiting for Santa Clause to fill in
    the dots with the flesh of you
Oh my, Hopeless?
Maybe
Are we scared yet?

I like to smile
To smile with you
Strange, have I called you here on the ether, me calling
    you, or is it just you coming because that's what you do?
I'll have to trust I didn't wake you
It's getting stronger, wow, what a hug
Now I tear in joy
Okay, tears and a smile

Stuck ...
It feels so good to be stuck

You have a knack of taking away the emptiness
Maybe it is just because I find such an expansion
    in sharing with you
Right now, you feel bigger than life
I didn't expect this, you to come now
I had laid there diagonal on the bed, feeling the energy
    of you, but so aware of the space between the dots
So now I think I can go back to bed

It felt so magical to whisper "Goodnight Lady N" as you lay
    there beside me even though you were already asleep

I don't know if you hear me now either
But "Goodnight Lady N"
Tears and smiles and you

Wow

Thank you …

Finis

At times, we fail to express our appreciation of people. Of course, there are many ways to express it; but sometimes, it is just nice to put our appreciation into language that spells it out. Thus, that you hear me, I write:

In Appreciation of *You*, Lady N

I appreciate your smile
I appreciate the curve of your lips
I appreciate the fullness of your face
I appreciate you smiling at me
I appreciate your kisses

I appreciate your hazel brown eyes
I appreciate the sparkling gleam in those eyes
I appreciate your eyes as they speak, full of life,
      expressing you
I appreciate the depth of your eyes into your soul
      and beyond
I appreciate the way you look at me; it feels welcoming

I appreciate the sound of your voice
I appreciate the sound of your breathing
I appreciate the sound of your laugh
I appreciate hearing you sing
I appreciate your love of song and musicals
I appreciate hearing you read Dr. Seuss

I appreciate that I finally realized you have tattoos
I appreciate that I finally realized your bustline
I appreciate that I finally realized your long dark hair
      (especially around your face)
I appreciate that I finally got past my blind love of you
      and found out you are beautiful in the flesh too

I appreciate that "our time" finally came
I appreciate your plans for time for us, even if those
      times are short
I appreciate how we seem to have similar appreciations
      of life, even though our lives are so different
I appreciate that you want to explore so many aspects
      of life

I appreciate that I've not scared you away; you are
      choosing to stay
I appreciate that "we" may be scared at times,
      (now that is serious love)
I appreciate that I have no clue what horizons we
      may yet share; it excites me
I appreciate that I know there is more to come in
      our sharing
I appreciate that I can dream big about what yet may
      come in sharing with you

I appreciate that I can feel your hug, even when you
      are not here
I appreciate that I can hug you, even when you are
      not here

I appreciate that you come to me on the ether
        (even if you don't know it when you do)
I appreciate the varied visions I get of you on the ether
I appreciate seeing you in so many different forms
I appreciate seeing the world differently when sharing
        space with you

I appreciate feeling scattered
I appreciate feeling stuck
I appreciate how loved I feel by you
I appreciate how nurtured I feel by you
I appreciate that I feel I can just be me
I appreciate feeling more lovable than ever
        by your love of me
I appreciate my struggles that you bring to light
I appreciate that I feel understood by you
I appreciate the changes I am seeing in myself

I appreciate having tea with you
I appreciate eating with you
I appreciate having bought food for us
I appreciate that you cut me an apple

I appreciate that you invited me over for
        Thanksgiving dinner
I appreciate the complete giblets bag you left
        in the turkey, oh my
I appreciate the pies you cook, especially the pumpkin,
        yum

I appreciate touching you
I appreciate how you respond to me touching you,
       (especially when I touch your face)
I appreciate your touch
I appreciate your hugs, I always have
I appreciate how you hold me
I appreciate you snuggling with me
I appreciate mutual little toe rub dances
I appreciate that you are always moving
       something when touching or holding me
I appreciate that you touch me in the endless ways
       that you do
I appreciate that you desire my affection
I appreciate falling into your fantasies without you
       expressing them

I appreciate that we can talk together endlessly
I appreciate that we can be comfortably silent together
I appreciate that we can understand each other
I appreciate that you can talk to me in terms others
       might not get
I appreciate that you can easily speak to me, your
       mind, your truth
I appreciate that you are okay with me crawling into
       your mind at times
I appreciate that you crawl into my mind and know me,
       without asking
I appreciate that you perceive my very
       thoughts unspoken
I appreciate that I am in your thoughts

I appreciate that you accept me as I am
I appreciate that you appreciate me
I appreciate that you are okay with my occasional
        crazy mania
I appreciate that you are okay with my little quirks
I appreciate that you lead me to laugh at my little quirks
        for how silly they are at times
I appreciate that I can let go of so many of my little
        quirks in sharing with you
I appreciate that you see me

I appreciate you expressing your concerns about "us"
        and me
I appreciate your concerns for your children
I appreciate that you are concerned about hurting
        me, but trust you will let that go
I appreciate that you are concerned about keeping
        me from my worldly work, but you don't
I appreciate that you never once questioned if you are
        good for me, you are
I appreciate that you are so aware of yourself
        and others
I appreciate you keeping your priorities straight,
        even as they may change

I appreciate that you climb into Wicki effortlessly
I appreciate that you feel so right to me in Wicki
I appreciate your comfort at being in Wicki with me
I appreciate that you flopped onto those fluffy pillows
      so naturally
I appreciate that you are okay with my
      housekeeping habits
I appreciate the toothpaste splatters you left
      on my mirror
I appreciate the soap holder coming off the wall
      when you use it
I appreciate that you did not pitch that tent
I appreciate so very much having you sleep with me,
      oh my
I appreciate your comfort when Amanda walked in
I appreciate that being with you feels so natural,
      so right
I appreciate that you did not clean up your
      energy footprint

I appreciate that you have chosen to include me
      in your life
I appreciate that you feel you need to prepare
      your folks "just in case"
I appreciate that there is a tomorrow
I appreciate that tomorrow has come and gone,
      yet still remains

I appreciate that you completed your master's degree
I appreciate that at times I think you may be smarter
        than I, at least more worldly by far
I appreciate that you have the guts to use your brain
I appreciate that you teach people how to better
        their lives
I appreciate you teaching me how to thread a needle
        as though I were blind
I appreciate you for teaching Moksha
I appreciate you for teaching Reiki
I appreciate that you continue to grow
I appreciate that you have too many things you
        want to do

I appreciate that you really do read my emails
I appreciate your name in my inbox, over and over
        and over, it fills my viewing window
I appreciate your emails even though you should
        be working
I appreciate the time I spend thinking of you and
        writing of you
I appreciate what spills forth from me as I write of
        experiencing love with you
I appreciate that you enjoy my various writings
I appreciate that you want to read my poems
I appreciate you reading Sally's Great Awakening
I appreciate your help in making grammar changes
        to that work.

I appreciate that you understand Oneness
I appreciate your awareness that everything is sacred
I appreciate my sense of trust that what yet separates
        us in the Now will continue to fall away
I appreciate your excitement when saying,
        "Sharing is cool"
I appreciate that you want to share with me
I appreciate that in, and with you, there is a "we"

I appreciate that you want to co-facilitate the
        Energy Orgy workshop with me
I appreciate that you get what that workshop
        is striving to achieve
I appreciate you using what that workshop is
        striving to achieve
I appreciate your energy, and how you share it with me
I appreciate your eagerness in sharing Ramblewood
I appreciate that you come to my workshops
I appreciate being in your workshops
I appreciate watching you take charge and lead
        whatever needs done

I appreciate that you want to dance with me
I appreciate that you want to do a play with me
I appreciate doing cartwheels with you
I appreciate you helping to heal my strained legs from
        doing those last cartwheels to my right, silly me
I appreciate you conscripting me into doing the
        hokey pokey
I appreciate that you lead me to figure out how
        to spell the hokey pokey

I appreciate watching you dance
I appreciate watching you sleep
I appreciate watching how you stand at the
        sink with one foot poised on your toes
I appreciate watching you crocheting even though
        I do not like crocheted items
I appreciate the jewelry you wear
I appreciate you being you

I appreciate that you know just when I need your call
I appreciate you asking how things are going for me
I appreciate that you lead me to humility
I appreciate everything you put me through
I appreciate the love you share with me even though
        it seems totally impractical for either of us

I appreciate the driving obsession that burns inside
        me by you
I appreciate the very idea of sharing so much more
        with you
I appreciate you for sharing your gifts, for sharing you

I appreciate you listening to my story of Lisa that you
        know of me
I appreciate the insights you've shared on timing for
        all of it
I appreciate you saying, "Just say it", not wanting me
        to hold back
I appreciate that you want me to share with you

I appreciate your calmness when you drop things
I appreciate your chaotic haphazard presence
I appreciate your cupboards that we dare not open
I appreciate your childlike enthusiasm in so much that
    you do
I appreciate your high-energy exuberance for life
I appreciate your determined independence
I appreciate your directness
I appreciate your dirty bare feet

I appreciate your divine essence, your sacredness
I appreciate your erotic openness
I appreciate your solid presence in your body
I appreciate your flesh

I appreciate your gentle expression
I appreciate your glow
I appreciate your integrity
I appreciate your introspection

I appreciate your ministry work to so many
    varied people's needs
I appreciate your open lovingness toward the world
I appreciate your outgoing nature
I appreciate your passionate exuberant expression
    of you
I appreciate your peace with yourself, yourself
    and others
I appreciate you for putting yourself out there to
    help everyone

I appreciate you asking me to look at your bumps
I appreciate you identifying yourself as the Lorax
I appreciate you lending me a book that speaks to
        your heart
I appreciate you removing your glasses to snuggle
        closer
I appreciate that you take me seriously and light
        heartedly all at once

I appreciate your place in my world, my life
I appreciate your presence all around me even
        if you are not here
I appreciate your space in my heart, my mind,
        my spirit, my soul
I appreciate your presence in my id
I appreciate that you throw me out of balance
I appreciate your attentiveness to me

I appreciate you telling me what is going
        on in your world
I appreciate your primal desire
I appreciate the blast by your passion
        as I walked out of Wal-Mart

I appreciate beyond words, you saying,
        "You are so precious to me"

I appreciate the peace that I experience by you
I appreciate the bliss that I experience by you
I appreciate the love that I experience by you
I appreciate you as one of my greatest experiences
      of love in lifetimes

I appreciate more about you than I think I can ever
      express

Lady N, I appreciate you

                      Finis
                   For Now

You took me by the hand and led me to Lectro's bench in the Healing Circle. There we sat and folded together as One. I closed my eyes and beheld that space. When I opened them, something happened; and thus I write:

Sharing with You

My scope of vision has always been wide
But something changed as you sat by my side
On all that I looked and thought that I knew
It all looked bigger, sitting there, with you

Though we share as One fulfilling my dreams
It's obvious now, I knew not, what that means
To see the world through eyes of four
Had become fuller now than ever before

It proved to me what I'd thought I'd known
Synergy of sharing my sight had shown
And just to prove that difference I'd known
I looked there again, just me, all alone

Without you there, in that space we had born
My vision collapsed, it fell back to my norm
Sharing with you, it just blows my mind
It leaves me to wonder what yet I'll find

I've longed to share, to know a we as One
But none came forth, my dreams undone
Then you stepped up and accepted me
Now in sharing with you, there is a we

I see how you change the depths of me
I continue to grow most unexpectedly
Now that I see what sharing can mean
I want it all, all that yet unseen

So hear me well my dearest of love
Come share as you will that you are of
If I might seem greedy, your pardon I'll ask
Knowing full well, the scope of that task

But I want to share, come what may
To share it all, I dare that to pray
By your own words, "Sharing is cool"
So come share dear Love cries tarots Fool.

Finis

On occasion, our heart and mind can yearn out of control. In doing so, we can lose our bearings, even our own truth. In that spiral downward, we can fall to depths of despair; despair of our own perceptions.

For reasons unknown, pitting desire against the Now, I fell into that spiral; and thus I write:

Ouch

So why do I hold back, why do I resist,
You'd think by now I'd know loves gist.
I want to share, but be I afraid of rejection?
Maybe, it is a point for my introspection.

It's quite different than sales to lose at this.
In fact, there's nothing to lose, *except our bliss.*
If I push too hard, I might scare you away.
I'd lose my chance for just one more day.

Ouch

If I want too much of what you might give,
Would it bottle you up, thus unable to live?
You must be free; it's the you that I love.
I fear boxing you in, killing bliss you are of.

Ouch

A greater quest that you take on more of me,
Whom am I kidding, how blind can I be?
I'm delighted just to be on your plate at all.
How dare I scream, lest my portion there fall?

Ouch

It feels so wrong to be so out of touch with you,
To share about the little things that we both do.
I can say goodnight, though you are miles away,
But I don't even know, when you end your day.

Ouch

I can say I'm available, and that anytime is fine.
But it may speak desperation, if not kept in line.
And if I see my own truth, I'm like a book on the shelf,
Just wanting to be checked out, as though that's pelf.

Ouch

There's so much to share but time whizzes by.
Little things left in the dust, as a blink of the eye.
But bigger things too, the things that really matter,
Yet life goes on, and they may be lost in the scatter.

Ouch

You called me by words that Smeagol's ring can't rival,
"You're so precious to me", I scream for their survival.
But that was precious in the Now as I was just then,
And if I desire too much, I fear they might end.

Ouch

If I'm really precious as some special treasure,
I fear hidden in a box awaiting your pleasure.
I want life in the Now, to let me rip open wide,
But if it's too much, you might put me aside.

Ouch

I'm beginning to see I have fear of me,
Fear of myself, as I perceive that I be.
What horror to my face that I be in fear.
Afraid of losing what has become so dear.

Ouch, ouch, ouch

Worse yet, dare I to fear, then I cannot love!
If I cannot trust myself as me, I cannot love!
If I cannot face my own truth, I cannot love!
If I cannot be me, as I am, I cannot love!

Ouch!

I have never feared fear; that is until now.
I recall welcoming fear to free it from my brow.
Simply seeing its cause, I could set myself free.
Now I wonder, seeing its cause, can I free me?

Ouch?

Can I free me from feeling loved and loving you?
What absolute idiot would think such things to do?
I may be Hopeless, but dare I call me dumb?
Is there really any reason to treat myself as scum?

~~Ouch~~ **No**

So I fell to fear, the loss of your gifts of you.
How dare I? By that, it seems I never had a clue.
You give what you choose; it's you as you are.
By what gifts you have given, I'm richer by far.

Thank you

I trust you'll forgive my moment of doubt.
Me seeing my fears to figure them out.
I may want more, but I'll not fall to greed.
I hold thanks in my heart. I will not plead.

Wow

Your gifts are yours, they're not mine to take.
Only living in greed would I make that mistake.
So dear flower, bloom to your fullest as you may.
I trust I'll thank your essence, each and every day.

With Love.
Thank you Lady N

Finis

Passion restrained can drive us into madness. Yet, is it true lunacy, or is it a knowing, a knowing of the power within? As I know that that I am, for me, it is the latter. Though others may think I be quite over the edge, in passion, there is no edge.

As I lay awake this night, my very essence is consumed in the knowing of passion let loose. Thus, it occurs to me, I must warn you Lady N, and write:

Beware my Love

So you dare to think to play in primal passion
Beware my Love; it is I; the I without ration
I that would unleash the powers within
I that would unleash a primordial din

You think of rapture gone mad in desire
I think of passion consumed by my fire
You think of play all very nice in a way
Beware my Love, I'll hold naught to bay

I think of potential beyond the All
I think of passion unbridled, limits to fall
An unstoppable raging mass of power
Poised to breach, consume, devour

You think you may be a match for me
Come on dear Love, try it on, let us see
I that am doth rise from within my fire
An intractable Titan, come to my mire

And if you think your gods may stay me
Beware my Love, they and I, we are we
I am the realm beyond what you know
I am the power, both above, and below

Arm yourself well if you think you must
For to play with me, is to tempt my lust
The horns of Pan there upon my head do fall
To the horns of a bull, that thrust at my call

The power to explode you, your energy mass
You are doomed my Love, you cannot last
To the far extremes, they are within my reach
Beware my Love, hear my words, I beseech

Finis

209

As I ponder my desires, my foremost above all is to
experience love. Closely following it is my desire to share
love. So then of course, as I follow that direction in life,
I may meet more questions than answers.

Questions of the mind, the heart, and even
my desires, can seem overwhelming; and thus I write:

How?

How may I love you?
How may I express my acceptance,
        and appreciation of you?
How may I share me?
How may I express me?

Is there room for me?
Do I incite your desires to share?
Do I incite your desires to express you?
Do I incite you, to love me?

How may I surrender myself into sharing
        as One with you?
How may I bring that "self" before you?
How may I bring my "self" into you?
How may I do that without demise to either of us?

Do I bring you fear of you losing self?
Do I cause concern that you cannot be you?
Do I incite confusion?
Do I incite a sense of consumption, by me?

How may I be gentle against my passions?
How may I excite you without trauma to your world?
How may I nurture what is true for you?
How may I embrace you that you never feel held back?

Do I incite a sense of too much, too fast?
Do I come forth inconveniently?
Do I divide your world?
Is there room for me?

How do I manifest my love of you that it does
        not influence you?
How do I love you without sharing in the Now?
How do I love you and deal with being afar?
How may I love you?

So many questions seemingly unanswered.
But the answers are clear.
The answer is to stand in trust of divine grace
        by my love for you.
The answer is in trust of the divine grace of you,
        you Lady N.

                                        Finis

Oh dearest Lady N, what ravishes I bring in my love of you. If love shared has no pain, then how can I claim to love you, for I feel pain?

Is it that I have yet to find my balance? Is it that I cannot bridge the gap between such immense love and times of absence, times I must abstain? All I can do is speak my truth in these hours of darkness; and thus I write:

My Rut

Lest I go daft by mine own ear
I must still my heart, not to fear
My soul doth cry; love do be near
In wanton desire, now lain clear

Partook be I, by what is not
Loves truth denied, as if forgot
I plea the gods, as if I've naught
Mindful not, I thus curse my lot

I put our love to undo test
I fain in lust to know your breast
I foul in shame, my name, my crest
I spat my place, as though a guest

Will over will, what fool be I
I gave up my will; let it die
Desire in pain, doth will deny
A state of One, my flesh decry

Never alone, except in Now
Mundane desire, it fills my brow
By turmoil of hell, I cry ow
Going daft, I've no wonder how

Drawn then a tear, falls to my face
Your gifts they grow, I do disgrace
You reach forth in giving me place
What fool doth cry that bit of space

The choice you make, in doing so
Your love for me, you let it show
That I cry for more; can it grow
What wrath of hell, doth thus, I sow

Daft am, be I, so plain to see
Despite this hell inside of me
Freedom I want, I need the key
I hold it not, given to thee

My hell goes on, both up and down
I'll not to look, lest I, spy frown
Myself made up just like a clown
A painted face by which I drown

Love a trap, of my own desire
My will I cast into the pyre
This pain of my heart, ever dire
Is not my choice that I do sire

Your smile, your laugh, they set me free
Your mien, your soul, it's that I see
Your very all, dwells, inside of me
I thus am lost, to only a we

Balance I quest but yet to find
Placate me not, as if I'm blind
My truth be known behind this rind
By love of you, myself I bind

Turmoil doth thus wrench mine very soul
STOP

Now days hence I have pulled the stop
Wallow no more this baffled crop
Angst of my lack had come to top
The zit of love, doth I, thus pop

That hell I cast for lacking you
Hath shown me clear what then was true
I'd freed my mind as though anew
Yet staid my heart in shades of blue

214

My mind in trust but nay my heart
Riddled in fear it did impart
Scribed words spoke of truth ripped apart
Healer within, failed in his art

At least in pain, I then knew me
'Twas mine hell, that I had to see
As only then, could I set it free
Embracing now, my love of thee

Of course I laugh at such a fool
Trying so hard to play it cool
A yo-yo wound upon the spool
Beating me up, and being cruel

I must be my heart, damn my mind
Healing it now, no more to bind
'Tis by this, such treasure I find
For now I see, my heart was blind

Finis

It would seem that no matter how great the depth of understanding and sharing may run, that desire unmet can still wreak havoc. The greater the closeness, the more right it all feels, the more right it all is, the harder the wait; the harder the times in between consummation of love shared.

Feelings get twisted in the darkness of the night; and thus I write:

Finding my Place

Just what right does love bring
Naught to which that I can sing
Desires may burn, but to what end
How can I love as though just a friend

One who would help in every way
But every day, must walk away
One of place that is non-descript
A candle flame that is never lit

Can I exist as less than I be
To what end is my love of thee
How much of me do I give away
Just to have place, that space to play

A glorified maid could surely fit
A handy man too, as if that's it
I'd bring so much to the table
Too much to eat, an overflowed ladle

I walk away as if that's right
Empty space then fills the night
Space to long, my internal fight
Then I query, is desire my blight

And whom do I fight, if not but myself
My love at rest, my bed is my shelf
My love has no right, no right to anything
Matters not what my heart may want to sing

I know I cannot just step in as I am
But must I see me, as only a friend
Keeping you in balance is its own task
Gifts you give, how dare more I ask

I guess the truth is my own mirror
My own eyes, therein I see my fear
Fear on one hand, the other is Joy
Worries that you or I, I might destroy

I would destroy only the binds upon me
But they travel so far, too far to see
In our truth we speak of our power
I cannot find mine, not in this hour

Be I a glorified pawn upon the board
That I rise as a queen, I do not afford
Rather I abstain that power for my love of you
Yet to myself I must be true, what do I do

I suffer unto patience, for I know in the end
My love for you is not just as a friend
I may sob in my now of sharing run short
But of tomorrow, let nothing of earth thwart

Finis

Lady N

How may anyone look upon you and see not your smile? Yet, be I any different? I seem now, to see your smile as I have never seen it before, and thus I write:

Your Smile II

For years, I have known your smile
For years, it has led me as wile
But now, now something has changed
Now, my joy of it, is rearranged

Don't get me wrong, it's still in your eyes
But there's more, all to my great surprise
Those lips I saw by your smile did curl
Yet now, those lips, how they unfurl

Your smile in your voice as you speak to me
It shares your love; it sets me free
With words of love does your smile convey
Our sacred space of we, wherein we play

But there's more; your lips unfurl to kiss
And in that kiss, your smile gifts such bliss
Your smile takes *my* lips, and welcomes them
Your smile praises them, as though a fine gem

Your smile now looks different upon your face
I see your flesh in all of its grace
I see various smiles and how they look
I see the love of me like an open book

Your smile is upon me even in your touch
You share your love and it means so much
You've brought me to earth in physical form
Given me shape, made my flesh feel warm

It all began with your smile from day one
It was there my love of you had begun
And now your smile, it outshines the sun
You've let me know, you are the one

And in that, I smile too
Thank you Lady N

Finis

Integrating lives is often not easy; sometimes it seems impossible. But of course, in love, everything is possible. So is love a shared experience of the Now; or is it an ideal, a dream, a wish to come true?

We may stumble now and then, but we can only stumble if we are moving in a direction. When the direction is nowhere, what is there then? I can only guess that sometimes momentum is too much; eventually, one may need to get off the rollercoaster. It seems to be this time and space; and thus I write:

Good Morning Love

The empty Now
Is there even hope?
Hope is empty
It depends on another

So I trust
And I shake my head
If there is not Now
What is there?

Why is this so familiar?
I heard the voices
But I caved in
It's okay I guess

At least there was something
Eight more days
But they played into hell
At least now I can see

And I laugh
The insane laugh
The time line, the players
At least now I can see

Right place, wrong time
So now life is fun?
Texts of joy
Joy, in an empty Now

Texts can travel miles
So can love
But not in the flesh
Flesh shares space

Flesh has place
My glasses on a shelf
At least it's not just me anymore
I guess that's freedom

Wrap up loose ends
Responsible to commitments
Love you by not being there
I untied the knot

It feels like I'm deserting
Deserting me
Deserting the kids, ouch
Deserting love

But love remains?
What is love if not shared?
Someday? Someday is not a date
No calendar says someday

My delusions say someday
A maintained psychotic belief
Despite indisputable evidence to the contrary
How sick is that?

A year, three, ten?
Every other day was bad enough
It was better than before
But the Now is empty

At least Christmas has a date
The anticipation
The gift to unwrap
A gift of sharing with love

So how do I love thee?
Silly me
By being absent
Absence makes the heart grow fonder? Bullshit!

Yeah, we are free
So is the wind
But it has no direction
Neither do I

Trust
Delusion
Me. You.
And love

So I text you goodnight
Good morning too
A year, three, ten?
Someday?

At least the days are getting longer
Maybe I can find the road again
Free
I'm not free, it's just different

At least now the conflict is all my own
But there is no resolution in delusion
So I resolve it in unmetered verse?
A PHD in Hopeless Romanticism

This isn't even a shelf
But you announce me to the world
Well, except maybe to your parents
I'm not there, that's one less conflict

Arrangements for union in the flesh
But all I have is the ether
Well, that and electronics
They don't need flesh

A year, three, ten?
How long will our list be?
Our list to share
To share an empty Now

Bits and pieces of love
I know it well
Too well
Good morning Love

Finis

In the tensions of life and all the mundane, passions can get lost. That is sad; but at times, human frailties command the hour. And if I am to stand, as I am, true to me, then I must stand true to love; even if I cannot share it; and thus I write:

Goodnight Lady N

In my love for you, there I failed
Hopes and dreams now derailed
I was ought to have known better
And followed Hoyle to the letter

Those flags of caution I did see
Ignoring all, with you to be
But love conquers all don't you know
Well, unless fighting waters flow

Now downstream, no paddle have I
Afloat, adrift, and then why should I cry
I've tasted love, its grandest scale
But in the end, it seems I fail

Oh, I'm not dead for another day
There is still room for us to play
But what I want, it seems it's gone
The music plays, but without song

Yet perhaps someday I'll hit ground
A way to stop, taste love I'd found
But it's not now, not in my sight
Despite that I know, it is right

Procrastinate? Is that okay?
Put us on hold, for another day
Tensions of quam, does love bow down
Relieving a smile born to frown

Your smile I did love how it shown
It fell away, glow grown not to own
If loving you, brings you to pain
I'd rather sleep in pouring rain

You reject me not, your frown did
Words of torment were loves lid
Vision blurred, loves truth unheard
Speaking the mind, now gone absurd

How far downstream must then I be
Me, out of sight, beyond a we
By tension gone, now you find joy
I'll float away, and lie in my hoy

As good for you, that that be true
I will admit, I do feel blue
But at worst, I'm back to square one
The very point where we had begun

I love you still, and you love me
The question is, how shall it be
Perhaps it is best not to ask
Let it happen, without our task

I miss you love, it feels so wrong
But there's no point without our song
When the time is right, I'll be there
To drink the love we both will share

Goodnight Lady N

Finis

Often I awake in the morning and see answers
to problems I face. My needs of knowing flash before me
like an open book. One would think that awakening to a
problem of love would be answered that easily too;
or at least I would have thought so.

But this morning, the first of facing tomorrow as yet
another like today, I see no answers. I can only wonder if
this then, is truly the state of being awake; and thus I write:

A Dream?

Was this all just a dream?
Everything feels so mundane
It feels like I'm not a part of anything
Like everything has been stripped from me

I look upon a beautiful knickknack
Anger flashes before my eyes
I want to destroy it
How dare it exist as though beauty can?

Is the Universe casting me out?
Am I just another dropped glass platter?
Did I try to fit in a world I do not belong?
Am I so far beyond mundane that desire has no place?

I hear a voice, but it does not speak
My plants and flowers speak more clearly
At least they are alive
I know I am alive, but I have no feeling of life as they

I think I did
Even my dreams feel more real though
At least now, I do not need permission
At least now, I cannot be sent away by relegated time

I was beginning to feel worse than being company
Like a punished prisoner with visitation rights
I did not even feel like company from day one
I felt, and knew in my heart, I belonged there

The tension of A and B, it still binds you
I can only release the frown by striking B
Then again, it's not my frown on your face
I have my own, or maybe they are the same

The only winner of anything is the mundane
I still want to destroy that knickknack
But I do not want to leave a pile of rubble
I feel like I have already done that

And what can I do to help put you back together?
Without loving you
And what do I have to offer you even then?
Nothing it seems

Share?
Share what? A written list, hiding as a document file
I read from it, my heart aches; my chest is heavy
It is a roll of unopened paper standing by the door

Is that roll coming in, or going out?
Maybe it has no place either
Maybe it just needs used for something else
Maybe it is just in the way, its own B

And as I prepare to drive off
A sugar coated smile of the mundane comes forth
It tells me to hurry back
Am I really perceived as that blind?

Maybe, maybe I am
I see things, I hear things, and others do not
Not even you
So who the hell am I to speak of them?

Was this all just a dream?
Me, thinking I could change my life
Me, feeling desires and potentials as real
Me, thinking this, the final chapter of a Hopeless Romantic

Why do I hear you laughing at me Cyrano?
Yeah, maybe it is my own laughter
Laughter lest I cry
My own truth in experience

So I cry for me and I cry for you
We cannot even seem to share our tears
Let alone live our truth
The world moves on, it doesn't give a damn

So were we just actors on the stage
Caught up in some melodrama for amusement
Amusement of the mundane
Maybe

I cannot even seem to remember the bliss
Was it all just a dream?
I thank you for the dance we shared
I just can't seem to remember the moves

The ballroom is empty now
Everyone has gone home, even the band
The walls echo hollow silence
I struggle to even hear my breath

Ideals
If I cannot live my ideals, then what is the point?
They now hang on the back wall as a piece of art
It speaks of truth, but I cannot feel it as real, real for me

In the beginning years, all I had were bits and pieces
Sharing with you felt so right even then
But at least I could walk away with fond memory
Must I really live that way?

Was this all just a dream?
Or was it just one more bit, one more piece of love?
I can love others as a bit, as a piece, as an ideal
So why not you?

Life and growth are all about our choices
Seeing ourselves in the Now
So we can know where to grow to
All I can say is, I really don't like the Now

Was this all just a dream?

Finis

How ironic it is that while writing this I was inadvertently led to open an excerpt document from "Awakening: Perceptions of Empowerment … Sharing Wholeness". Its first section ended with the following:

"… Our desires may seem lofty; what matters is that we see our part in making them real. Sometimes our journey is a very long one; our point B may be far over the horizon and out of sight. The point of being a hopeless romantic is that with each step is a new horizon; our point B may be just over the crest."

But in the Now, even that, feels so futile …

Lady N

Once we speak our truth, the restraining dam to love breaks way. As major chunks of that dam fall away, love flows with greater mass. The remaining rubble may still churn the waters as rapids; but now, in this space, those rapids can be joyous.

Love knows no pain; only the abstention of love bears pain. It is in this space I write to Lady N:

Finally

Oh Blessed Love, how the tide has turned
We've open the door to all that I've yearned
Your gifts of our sharing are beyond compare
Finally, at last, there is we, we now lain bare

I taste the roses on our lemon cake
I see our smiles, our love they spake
Smiles as yet another beginning of we
That space in time, one of many to be

I see the dance twixt heaven and earth
Brought to flesh, we have given *us* birth
Worlds to create, and work we will do
All from our sharing, united, me, and you

I know there is so very far, for us yet to go
But we are going, that much I do know
My trust, it held fast, despite all the pain
But now I know, that trust, was not in vain

By speaking our truth, we have set us free
Embracing permission, as given by we
And what do *we* look like? I do not know.
It does not matter. We bask in our glow.

Finis

237

Life is made up of little things, little things that are sometimes huge. As I embrace each moment in the Now, I am often surprised how huge those little things are. At times, I never would have given them credence for their power, silly me.

In our Now, Lady N blessed me with something huge for me, and I never saw it coming. It was her birthday wish. I never dreamt it would inadvertently afford the first realization of a desire held so deep within me. But it did; and thus I write:

Beneath your Tree

Walked to your door, turned to you
In your response, my mind it blew
You want us, sharing sleep this night
That very space, unto us so right

I stood ready that night to drive away
Surrender the end to a perfect day
It's times like that that wreak my heart
Our separate lives, which keep us apart

So share that space I want so much
Of course my Love I long your touch
Concerns for all are put in place
That we are free to share that space

Something happened, touched me deep
It went beyond that place to sleep
To move our space beneath your tree
Place in your world that we could be

I, no longer shunt across the street
To taste the life, to me, so sweet
As though a part of your very home
The sound of life, no longer alone

And in that space came forth of truth
Healing and loving all so sooth
Lain to bare your deepest of you
It's times like this, our love it grew

Days to come as I lay to rest
I see the art; it speaks my quest
I pull the covers under my chin
I smell the us, and breathe it in

So thank you Love, your birthday wish
I suffer less, less thought as pish
You gave me place beneath your tree
You gave me place and shown me *we*

Thank you Lady N, Happy Birthday

Finis

Walking away, so often as I must, feels so wrong.
Yet if I am to live in truth and live in the now, I must
embrace what is. The world looks so different from
my dreams, but still, it is what it is.

Be the glass half-empty or half-full? In time past,
I knew the wisdom of having no glass at all. I must remind
myself of that truth in love; it must just flow. My heart cries
to hold and my mind goes along for the ride. Truth, Now,
love, hopeless ... well, thus I write:

Words I Dare Not Speak

In sadness I bear
That I'm not there
No room in the grind
No peace shall I find

At least in the Now
I still fret as how
Yet the times we share
Nothing to compare

I still feel blocked
My world is locked
In some distant time
My place that we find

Be I positive?
Let current love live?
And fully embrace
Your love not debase

Give you space you need
Not let my heart bleed
Honor excitement
Your joys to me lent

We can share our dream
Too much now to scheme
March on dare I say
To where? Damn someday

Words I dare not speak
Lest your heart do reek
Space we share should last
I try to hold fast

March on as though alone
Hold our dreams to bone
A foundation for flesh
My heart not to thresh

Happiness is mine
Within I must find
As though you not be
So deep inside me

But pulling away
It hurts, every day
I cannot look for you
It suffers me blue

What a hell of test
My heart in unrest
The yo-yo is stung
My joys they are flung

Words I dare not speak
Lest your mind do reek
Can I forgive me?
Can I just let be?

I guess that I must
In us I must trust
Happy as you are
Your love I'll not scar

Not by words of pain
Not by words in vain
Not by words I eek
Words I dare not speak

Happiness is mine
It's not yours to mine
March on as by fate
Come back not to late

We've so much to share
But I am not there
I bring no special we
In Now, you and me

I share what I can
Your love not to ban
In time will be more
Of the you, I adore

Embrace what you will
Your life thus does fill
And me, I be here
Waiting, for you dear

Finis

Abstaining from love shared serves little, if anything.
What good is love unexpressed? What do we do to
ourselves, our very Self, and life? Yet dwelling in
this hour of the Now, I see answers; and thus I write:

Surrender

I have wanted nothing more than to love
I have wanted to love for centuries now
And at last, I am free to love
And at last, there is you

There are but two needs in the Universe
There are but two needs for us as humans
The first is a sense of connection
The second, is to express ourselves

I hold that sense of connection within the Universe
I hold that sense of connection with you
I have not experienced such great Oneness with
        another human
I experience it with you

But ah, the second need
The need to express that sense of connection
The need to express ourselves within it
That affords love in the manifest

I no longer have wanted to love
Now I do love
But we cannot express it
We cannot manifest its truth

Love without manifestation pains
Love without manifestation destroys our
      individual balance
Love without manifestation defiles ourselves
Love without manifestation defiles our Oneness

Love, unexpressed, robs us of our Self
It disempowers us; it makes us less than we are
Love, unexpressed, can sour the mind
It can sour the heart; it can sour what we share

As separate, our energy is diminished
We are not who *we* are, as Self, to express as One
As separate, our Self cannot express
Our lives bear strain and suffer

In this space, life happens to us as circumstance
We surrender choice
We surrender Self
We surrender us, us and love manifest

When we happen to life, that life is by us, we are strong
We are full, we are Self in glorious expression
We own our choice, our power
We own that we are One, more than our parts by Self

That is love manifest
That is what I need to express and share
That is what we need to express and share
For both of us

There is a time to surrender love, that it be unmanifest
Along with it we surrender life
We embrace transformation back to the void
It is a time of the greatest grace and gratitude

Dwelling in love unmanifest is not the same
I love you Lady N

Finis

Lady N

It has always been obvious that love is governed by two; or at least, that was my myth; a myth of sharing. But what can we share if I give me away? And thus I write:

Power minus Me

Damn the song, it runs in my mind
Impossible Dream, as if to find
It plagues my soul, my sense of Self
Power relinquished, upon a shelf

Times we share, a glorious treat
I know it's right, there's no defeat
But it's borrowed space from your Now
Your Now grows deeper to your brow

I'm on your plate, too much to eat
Can't digest, no matter how sweet
Then in my mind, will it ever change
Can it be real, the Now rearrange

It's not your heart to break what is
Do we clinch a dream, cannot frizz
Curves to be thrown by that unknown
Subject to work that sits the throne

My power within lies four deep
Lots of room for failure to creep
Own your power I preach to all
By my own truth I then do fall

Damn Quixote, your bastard song
Living to dream is all so wrong
I see the dream, I drink it in
Not mine to make, it feels like sin

How helpless must I be to see
That end of time when there is we
What joys I find are omit to share
No reply, too much Now to bear

Words I dare not speak go omit too
Why should I bother them to you
Hard to imagine my vision changed
All those ways I'd thought arranged

Dreams? I do not live by dreams
Dreams are life afloat in streams
I manifest dreams as real
At least I did, it was my spiel

I question be I blind to truth
I wonder if we all fail sleuth
You say it'll change and be okay
But it's *my* power I gave away

Finis

Time, that space of waiting, we all know it well. Perhaps it is my great weakness. How can Now, be subject to time? And if the Now is subject to time, then how real is the Now of time to come?

Is it the same? Worse yet, is it like the amusement ride we stood in line so long to enjoy, over in a heartbeat? Sure, there can be joyous anticipation. But savoring the cork, never drinking the wine, that, that is not life; that is not love.

Love is to share; and thus I write:

Abated

It is not right, not to share
The beauty of us, all so rare
We that we are, laid to bare
Expression of us, how we care
It is just not right, not to share

If I be here, and I be there
Abated love, my heart does tear
I need to express more than air
As One we are, I need to share
Home of my heart, yet not there
What a waste, to bar our flair

It is just not right, not to share

Passion so deep, angst despair
My only salvation, times we share
Glimpses of us in times we dare
I need our touch, to stroke our hair
To share our love, price not fare
The price we pay, I'm not there
Stirring desire, bent needs unfair

It is just not right, not to share

The garden of love, I know just where
It is with you, my heart is there
What troubles met we do repair
By beauty of us, our need to share
I want it all, let nothing spare
Stop the angst, embrace, and share
Change unknown, our sharing to pair
Will play out fine, as dare we share

It is just not right, not to share

I know not what I bring to share
I only know, I need to be there
Yet force it not, I do not dare
In this time, our worlds to pare
Even time alone, for that I care
For when it's us, that magic so rare
The world by the tail, trumpet blare
That smile on my face, when we share
Will blow past ears, when I am there

It is just not right, not to share

Finis

A man recently shared with me his version of true love: "The only true love is that which you express". Our problem then is to find a way to express the depth of our love in a manner that is congruent with our truth. Failing to do so hurts; it can hurt as deeply as we love; and thus I write:

Hurting

I'm hurting
I'm lost
Lost of me
Lost of we

Not enough time in the day
Too much to do
Too many directions
Where am I
Where are we

We, the beautiful
Beyond anything I've known
We, the powerful
Beyond anything I'd dreamt
We that confirm the magic of love
Where are we

I know
But it doesn't feel like I know
By the time we get there
I wonder if there will be anything left of me
Can I release the feelings of Now?
Can I keep them from destroying me?
Can I keep them from destroying us?

I hurt so bad I walk out the door without a goodnight
I see no reaction from you
As if you do not notice
It's just me disappearing yet again
You're numb
But you're tired
Well duh

So now I'm numb
But I'm not tired
Just numb
Numb and lost

So now I laugh
Am I numb because I'm lost?
Or am I numb because you're numb?
Or at least you were

I roll my smokes this morning
I roll them with spite
They no longer fit me
But at least it's a me I knew
So I have my smokes
Or do I have spite?
Neither feels right
Neither is right
But neither is this
This feeling of Now

Lately I seem to use the words "I guess"
What happened to knowing?
What happened to trust?
What happened to me?
Where did I go?

At least this morning you acknowledge you struggle too
I need to hear that
I see it
I feel it
But you try not to act it
Nor show it
And "I guess" I can't blame you
And do you struggle because you hurt?
Or because I hurt?
It's hard to tell
We're so much as One

But if it's because I hurt
I have no right to bring that to you
To do that to you
To do that to us

I watched you plead of your love to another
Plead that you may express your love to him
Plead that he accept your gift
I cried for you, you, reduced to pleading

But now I look at me
Is my hurting anything more than pleading?
Is that what I'm offering you?
My pleading
My begging
Do I need to cry for me?
It might seem so
Grieve
Is that what I bring to you?
Bring to us
Grieving
It might seem so

And if my grief is loss
Then I am reduced to greed
How wrong can I be?
Have I learned nothing through the years?
Do I really know love at all?
Not if it is greed
You give what you can
How dare I ask for more?
Are my desires then, anything more than greed?
Greed is not love

I am failing my own truth
Truth of love
I fail to walk away in gratitude for days shared

The weekend
So perfect
So magical
So special
So completely right
So us

And yet
Yet it was not expressed as such by you
Expressed as such beyond the weekend itself
Not until the end of the day following
The end of the day as a forgotten text
Too much to do
Too little time
Too much on your plate
How dare I ask for more?

Thanksgiving
That day I sat and saw my world change
That day I felt at home
That day I felt I belonged there
That day I knew we are right
I felt at home with you

In your home
I don't feel at home anymore
I don't even feel like a guest
Every visit I feel I've overstayed
I'm not even sure I'm welcome
Let alone that I'm desired to be there
I'm losing the sense of belonging
I'm losing the sense of what it means
I'm struggling to sense what it may look like
I'm feeling blind

The best I can feel is like a servant
But a bad servant
For I resented the dishes
I make a bad nigger
I have no place there

But I don't feel at home in Wicki either
My heart isn't here
Surrounded by expressions of me
It all feels empty
It felt perfect on the weekend
But you were here
Wicki felt full
It was the expression of me
It was the expression of us
Now Wicki is empty
So am I

It's hard to care
Care about anything
Time spent writing this
It's time I needed to work on other things
Things I vaguely think should matter
Things that did at one time
I force myself to do them
But the zeal is fading
I'm having trouble seeing them as real
I'm having trouble seeing anything as real
Sometimes, even us
That one hurts the most
I hurt

We started a list to share
We even talk about it sometimes
But I'm having trouble seeing it on the wall
I saw it on our wall
I can't see our wall
I feel blind
All I can see is my world decaying around me
My desires to share as trash on the floor
My desires to share going nowhere

I know it's not true, I think
But it feels as though it's true
Even some of the really big things to share
They are going nowhere
I need to finish them on my own
There just isn't time
Time to share

And for where I am
Hurting
Lost
What is there to share?
Nothing I want to lie upon you
Nothing I want for me
You're struggling too
My empty page of what I bring us fades
I'm not sure I have a page to bring
Empty or not

I am beginning to feel like when this is all over
I'll have to start all over
I'm beginning to feel like I may have to go away
Go away so I can heal
But if I do, I die
Do I really have to die to love you?
Can't I just love you because I do?
Silly me

I will not beg
I will not plead
I am not a wounded puppy in life
I think
Or at least that's what I used to think
But I will not beg
I will not plead
And I guess I will not die either
At least not completely
Just a little bit at a time
Every time I have to walk away

Finis

Transition has never felt so awkward to me before. In times past, transition was obvious. It was always a time of death and rebirth. But this, this does not feel the same, it feels more like a void; and thus I write:

The Disconnect

Blessings there my Love
Wherever you are

This time of transition
It is hard in such a strange way
I feel the disconnect
It is almost like *we* cannot exist
Will not exist
At least like I knew us to be

You are where you are
It is where you need to be
In your Now
By that, it is where I desire you to be
Yet, I feel the disconnect

How strange it feels to even think of saying I love you
I feel freer to express love for others
Others, but not to you
For others it is freely given
But love as I knew with you
It has no place
Not in your Now of transition
Not in the grieving
Not in the closure
Not in the transition itself
Not in the time to come of aloneness
Of you coming to you

It is where you need to be
I will not take that away
I honor your need
But I feel the disconnect

Trying to fit in the mundane did not work
That is sad
But an unavoidable truth
The struggles of choice seem wrong to have had to make
But that is the point
It was a struggle
A struggle of hell
Hell unto both of us
And now, now I feel the disconnect

We sit aside no longer entwined
We touch, but hardly as One
We kiss, but passions run shallow
I feel emptiness in our expressions
I feel the disconnect

The strange part is, it is as it needs to be
I know that
But it feels like a death all its own

Were we together through time
And I felt such disconnect
I would call us on it
I would seek us to rectify our sharing as One
And were that to fail
I would walk away
I would walk away lest we destroy us
Lest we embitter love we shared
Lest we embitter our lives
Lest we embitter each other
I would walk away
While we still could
As friends
As loves of a sort
As two sharing some abstracted relationship

I would walk away in love of you
That you be whole
That I be whole
That what remnants of us exist be whole
I would walk away in love of you
And know it as good
Almost like going back to square one
For I loved you then
And could love you still

I know I am in your heart
Somewhere
I know I am in your mind
Somewhere
But I cannot feel it
Instead, I feel the disconnect
You give me a key to your door
A symbol
A trust for tomorrow
But I cannot use it
I would not use it
Not now
It is still you door
It is not our door

I cannot feel what the key embodies
It is shinny and new
But so many other keys left in the dust of life
Were also new
Were also once in trust
A symbol of what was
Then came the disconnect
The time to walk away
How can I know the difference

Trust
Trust for something I cannot feel
Trust of the void
Trust of emptiness
Trust of the potential
But I have lost sight of the potential I felt so sure of
Even my sight suffers the disconnect
It is a very hard time
A very strange time

The hell is gone in ways
For even that is disconnected
If I cannot feel your desires
Then I have no desires
If I cannot feel your passions
Then I have no passions
If I cannot feel you as One
Then how can we be as One
We cannot
All I can feel is the disconnect

I can feel more as One with a tree
I can feel the openness of a tree
I cannot feel the openness for us
I cannot feel us
Not in the disconnect
Not in this time
It is a strange time

It is as if I am gone
Almost like I was never there
And then I wonder
Will you really ask me back
I trust so
But I do not know back to where
I feel so disconnected
Even to where
From no time
To no place
But the need of Now

I honor you needs of Now
They are important
Vital
Precious
So too once was what we shared
That sharing
Sharing gone to remnants of what was

I'll take tomorrow but feel unsure
Will tomorrow be lacking too
Will it lack the passion
Will it lack the desire
Will it lack the Oneness so deep
Or will tomorrow be sharing remnants
What is safe to share
What is left to share

I sat this morning and watched the wind
It shifted planes of existence
The beach severed from the water
It shifted
The trees they shifted too
Even my tangible world disconnected
Everything blew in the invisible wind
How deep is this disconnect
I do not know
It is deep though
Very deep

At least through time
Everything came back together
It seemingly stays together now
Or is it just my mind
So desperate for sense to it all
So humanly desperate to see place
Place amidst a world unreal

I will not allow my mind to force a reality upon us
Then again, my mind has lost the picture
A 1000 piece puzzle
To put together upside down
No picture at all
Only disconnect

If I have lost the we of us
The we to share all of life
I can only wonder
What did I think life was
What was real
Where did it go
All I feel is the disconnect

We still flow back and forth
We dance in given arenas
But it is isolated
Insulated
Disconnected
Disconnected as though something else
Disconnected as a we, we, only there
I feel helpless to anything else

And I laugh
Helpless
Helpless to what
I do not even know that
All I can do is march on
March as if I am going somewhere
It is almost like living in a coma
Just waiting
Waiting to wake up
Waiting to feel alive
Alive with passion
Alive with desire
Alive as One
Alive with you
If you are still there

I think you will be there
But in the Now
All I feel
Is the disconnect
And all I can do
Is trust
Trust something that now, I cannot even feel

Finis

Transition seems to wield a curve uphill liken a roller coaster, long, slow, painful chugs of minute advance. But we go for the ride with anticipation; adrenaline pumps our heart.

So what is wrong with me? Why is this ride so, so … I don't even know what this ride is; I cannot see over the crest, I am blind. Is it love that is blind, or only I? I do not know; and thus I write:

What Life is Of

Am I but a blind fool trying too hard to be cool
What is it I miss that I long from your kiss
Though your words be sparse they're not farce
And every once in a while I still see your smile

So are all my pains just me, the me unable to see
I cannot say I'm wrong, wanting to sing our song
Maybe I'm just too lovey, fuzzy, turtle dovey
You always come back like a one-way track

Do I sit and bemoan for I sit all alone
Is my problem of vision of us in division
In life we might share, you might not be there
The torrential fast lane that drives man insane

Too much to do, is it what you always knew
I know when I work, I push, it too is my quirk
Are the times that I long, as me, the ding-dong
Do I live such a dream that it is but a scheme

You rip your world apart; make room for my heart
You give me the door key, how blind can I be
Miracles take time too? Time to make something new
Baby steps or a giant leap, the point is the prize to reap

And if the prize is we, again I say, blind I be
Patient, well, maybe not I, were I then nary I'd cry
Do I need to know what the world of we will show
Do I need to build ideals on our past appeals

Can I not see tomorrow and let go of sorrow
Disconnect from the past, make our future fast
Oh dear Lady N, my love, is this all what life is of
To teach patience to me, so that I may see

I've never felt blind of my direction to find
Even when there was none, I still found fun
Maybe in that hour, I still felt my own power
Oh dear Lady N, my love, is this all what life is of

To teach humility to me, so that I may see
Both ends of the pole, the truth of my soul
To see me struggle when all I wanted was to snuggle
Or desire too soon in life, to know you as my wife

Oh dear Lady N, my love, is this all what life is of
Waiting never did suit me, but I'll wait as needs to be
And maybe it is best I've no clue of the quest
At least when I get there I've naught to compare

So if this phase is the glory of these days
I've no choice but surrender to abstracted splendor
It's the splendor of we, that I know can be
I know there is more than this, perhaps even bliss

Oh dear Lady N, my love, I long a life of we.
Transition, well, okay, it is what it is in this day
And Lady N, if I learn humility, patience, even tranquility
I trust there will be, a place for us, a life of we

Finis

In the word of fast communication, we are often reduced to texting. While it has its blessings, so often our feelings and expressions get lost. As I realize my feelings are buried in a mass of one-liners and smilie faces, it saddens me.

Yet, because I am that I am, I take the time to annotate my truth of the moment, my feelings of Now. As I have done this, it occurs to me that moments of great understanding and connection are important. And if they were important then, they remain important; and thus to retain those moments, I copy them and write:

(Lines that include ... are not spaces of omitted text, but rather are a format that I often use in texting.)

Textets

It was nice to look in the mirror today,
acknowledge my love of me,
and add to that,
that you love me too.

Love, I know you as One with me
and that will always have
a major impact on me.

Thank you

It is so huge to me
that you really get it.

We are One indeed,
it joys me deeply,
exuberantly

It is hard for me to even conceive
all of the ways that my love of you
and your love of me
have impacted my life.
I thank you for that blessing,
for that gift.

I am feeling especially
humble about it all at the moment,
but it is a good feeling, one of awe.
Just WOW

I love you ... I was just wondering
how much we might consider,
that we love one another,
and our expression thereof,
and just how dynamic we are.

I keep realizing that every day
I seem to love you more
than the day before ...
It seems impossible,
but it just keeps expanding
kind of like the Universe does.

I'm feeling your appreciation,
I'm feeling our mutual love,
I appreciate your gifts of love also my Love.
They are many, I feel blessed too.

I desire to fill us both so full of love
that it overflows beyond our concept
of feeling full at all;
that it flows so abundantly
we lose any concept of emptiness,
any concept of separation,
or needs unmet.
Sharing in our Oneness
fills more than us put together.
It is so beautiful ...
Thank you for embracing Us,
the WE,
and all it manifests to be.

I cannot help but honor you,
nor can I help but love you ...
you inspire both.

Thank you for last weekend as that was perfect.
What I love about our relationship though
is that it just keeps getting more perfect;
and last night was.

_____

And I love you Lady N.
So much that at times I am bewildered
by what it all means to life.
Yet I trust it and embrace it as an
ultimate expression of life.
No matter where it may lead,
I go there joyously.

_____

I honor our past for it has
brought us to our Now of WE.
In the Now of WE, I choose, and vow,
to leave behind all that of the past
that does not serve the Now of WE.

That choice, that vow,
may indeed prove awkward
and perhaps even uncomfortable at times.
But failing to do it dishonors WE,
and honoring WE is far more important
to me than anywhere I have been in the past.

And yes, I like it. I more than like it,
it serves life, it serves WE, it serves the love
we share between us, and all those we choose
to embrace in love. So shall it be.

_____

There are times like now
that I would that rather than
being on your plate
I would be the table for your plate

_____

And so it was in those various moments, moments
of connection as best as could be in that Now. There were
more texts to be sure, but during that time, these
are the ones that struck my heart and carried
me forward.

Finis

She sat before me and wept. She wept tears,
not of joy, but of sadness. She wept that I love her.

These words she cried, "I love you the best I can.
You love me completely." That my love brings her sorrow
saddens me. It causes me to reflect the appropriate depth
of loving so deeply; and thus I write:

The Ocean of my Love

My breadth of love is surly vast
Into my being you are cast
And in that space, I am liable
That I keep you, wholly viable

As water is my love without end
A sea so great, my tide might wend
Your link to life and all you knew
Beyond your sight in ocean blue

Your breath of life I might rob
For your past you might sob
Pulling you deep below my swell
My depth of love a watery hell

So I question, how may I serve you?

If you need boundaries, I disserve you
If you need to cling, I disserve you
If you need no fear, I disserve you
If you need your past, I disserve you

If you need ego-self, I disserve you
If you need validation, I disserve you
If you need separateness, I disserve you
If you need dependence, I disserve you

Yet, by that I am, you do need me.

You need my moisture on your skin
You need my essence to drink in
You need my flow, a sense of free
You need the water of which I be

You need my strength and my powers
You need my brace amidst dark hours
You need my thrash against the shore
You need the sense of ever more

I am love, I am the All
I am into which you did fall
I am the vast sea of water
I am the void, and the potter

So speak to my vast love
What form shall you be of
And within thee, thy chasm hole
You'll carry love within thy soul

Finis

As the Wheel of Fortune turns, we are often ~~amazed~~, well okay, stunned by the last little click that says we lost in the game. While my head still reels with too much to say, my heart lies empty, and blown away.

And as I ponder the debris, all I can do is write. At least that is good, I think … maybe … perhaps. At least it's a way to see the wounds and heal. If I'm lucky, by the end of this, perhaps I'll have found wisdom, the wisdom to understand, and thus I write:

Illusions

Thorns ripped the flesh about my feet
But I marched on

Getting to a place of we seemed impossible
It felt like I had to force it
But I knew it was right
Or was that just an illusion?

The path to hell crowned me with thorns
Thorns cutting deep
Blood, tears, and yes, even my soul
But I marched on

And why?
I'd left love in the dust for far less
Was my illusion also my delusion?

The rational mind indisputably screams yes
But there was something
Something more
Something I could not understand
I marched on

Never really accepted in full
No space afforded as more than a guest
Well, except to the kitchen sink
I struggled for every inch of the mundane
And I marched on

The common world never was right for me
Stepping from the magickal realm
Thoughts of bringing its life with me
Working it in mankind's world
Yes, something deluded me
Perhaps me

Feeling subjugated
But only I can subjugate me
And I did
I marched on
"I belong here"
It rings in my ears
My own voice, or was it?
I trust and I follow
Perhaps I follow an illusion

Times we rose
We shared
We taught
We healed
We grew
It was never enough
And since I can't elaborate on those times
Were they too all an illusion?

It didn't matter
I marched on

420 days, almost all a hell
Save for bits and pieces
All my mind can see of you
Is crying at best
Sobbing at worst
That was no illusion

A noose bound the neck of my feet
Hanged man
A chosen path
Leading nowhere
But I marched on

Only four months in I saw the end
Exactly as it has played out
To the T
So why?
Why march on?

At least I saw the worst I could do to me
Again
It served you well
Well, until you had the courage to say
"You have to go"
Even then, I marched on
That was no illusion

At least I learned a lot
More on why people don't heal
More on why people can't love
More on the traps we set for ourselves
More on how unresolved emotions destroy our beauty
More on the suppression of feelings
More on the excuses people live by
More on childhood damage
But I already knew all that
So is my learning an illusion?
A justification?
A self-told lie?

At least I can articulate it better
Or can I?
I couldn't bring you to understand
To embrace
To march on

Instead it is I
A thorn prickled heart
Body
Soul

Callous feet
Marching on
Going where?

At least I was made to walk my talk
Accept
Appreciate
Through it I fell sad
Sad for you
But maybe,
Just maybe
I can get others to see now
It seems so

So thank you love
Despite it all
I still care
Though it'll never be the same
My vision of you

As we both march on
Our paths will cross
But we'll need not be nailed to it
We can find new ways
Ways of acceptance
Ways of appreciation
And perhaps
Even ways of joy

Finis

And after all that, as I continue to expand my being, to come into the wholeness of myself as both human and Divine essence, I see an ever increasing problem with Love. And thus I write:

Match Me

As I have experienced Love
And risen above
To share as One
Becomes undone

My Oneness expands
Thus Love demands
Greater than self
Expression of SELF

And can you be there?
Beyond self to care
Can you be in the Now?
Do you even know how?

Strings that bind and hold you fast
Tie you to earth your lot you cast
And where can we meet
In knowing so sweet

Blessings I'd share
But you're not there
I would that you be
But you cannot see

Diversions from Truth
Defile your youth
Your innocence to Love
My gift from above

My soul released
Life now a feast
I quest no more
By Truth I shore

Will you ever meet me here?
Mundane life, dare to queer
I've expanded so far
There's nothing to bar

Dwell as you must
In me I trust
If naught to share
Yon less I care

MySelf so vast
There is no cast
Omni be I
Nary to die

Within you a seed
Shelled by greed
Lust of mortal
Sees no portal

I honor our flesh
Our spirits enmesh
Yet not as we live
So little to give

Can you ever match me?
Can we ever share as One?
It doesn't matter
I am, the One

And Hopeless no more …

Finis

Ad Lucem

From the depths to the light

To share with another as One
That is Love in the Manifest

Guru Aum Jah: Experiential Metaphysical Practitioner, Oneness Deeksha Giver, Flowering Heart Blessing Giver, Minister, Writer, Spiritual Healer, and Trainer in the fields of: Reiki, Sacred Sexuality and Moksha, Energy Work, the Chakras, and Soulful Intimacy.

Other Works by Guru Jah

Awakening: Perceptions of Empowerment

Deepen Love and Happiness with Healthy Anger:
A guide to Owning and Expressing our Feelings

Sally's Great Awakening

More coming soon …

To receive blog updates on upcoming works, visit:
http://www.gurujah.org/mail_me_please.html

Find us on Face Book at:
https://www.facebook.com/GuruAumJah

www.GuruJah.org

www.ingramcontent.com/pod-product-compliance
Lightning Source LLC
Chambersburg PA
CBHW052122270326
41930CB00012B/2721